SONS OF ISHMAEL: *HOW SHALL THEY HEAR?*

Sons of Ishmael: How Shall They Hear?

**FINLAY
M.
GRAHAM**

CONVENTION PRESS / NASHVILLE, TENNESSEE

A publication of the
Foreign Mission Board
Richmond, Virginia

© Copyright 1969 • Convention Press
Nashville, Tennessee

522-213

Code Number: Church Study Course
This book is number 1015 in category 10,
section for Adults.

If requesting credit after 1971, ask for credit in category 1009.
Library of Congress catalog card number: 69-17887
Printed in the United States of America
100.JY696

Gift from First Baptist Church of St.Cloud $6.99

Contents

Contents

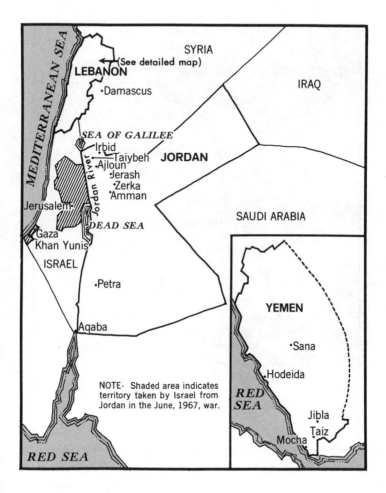

SYRIA

LEBANON

(See detailed map)

·Damascus

IRAQ

MEDITERRANEAN SEA

SEA OF GALILEE

Irbid
·Taiybeh
·Ajloun
·Jerash
·Zerka
·Amman

JORDAN

Jordan River

Jerusalem·

DEAD SEA

SAUDI ARABIA

Gaza
Khan Yunis

ISRAEL

·Petra

Aqaba

NOTE- Shaded area indicates territory taken by Israel from Jordan in the June, 1967, war.

YEMEN

·Sana

·Hodeida

RED SEA

Jibla
Taiz
Mocha

RED SEA

Introduction

Resplendent in its fresh covering of gold leaf, the Muslim shrine called the Dome of the Rock today catches the eye of Jerusalem-bound pilgrims traveling westward on the Jericho road. Passing through Bethany and overlooking the Kidron Valley, they catch their first closeup view of the Holy City. Coated for centuries with baser metals, the Dome was royally embellished a few years ago through the generosity of oil-rich Arab states. The site on which this striking monument stands is sacred to the three great monotheistic faiths: Judaism, Christianity, and Islam.[1]

To this place, the traditional Mount Moriah, Abraham brought his son Isaac to be offered as a sacrifice in obedience to the command of God. Here also, King David purchased the threshing floor of Ornan, the Jebusite, on which King Solomon built the Temple of Jehovah which was reconstructed by Zerubbabel after the Babylonian captivity and eventually outclassed in splendor by Herod the Great's magnificent edifice. Traditionally, Jewish worship centers in this sacred spot, although the Jews have not always held it.

To the Temple in Jerusalem, Jesus of Nazareth was taken as a baby to be dedicated to the Lord. There, at the early age of twelve, he confounded the religious leaders of his day with his profound questions. And the

Temple area was the scene of much of the Galilean Prophet's teaching in his later years. On a continuation of the same rock shelf on which the Temple was built, to the north on a hill called Calvary, this same Jesus was crucified for the redemption of mankind. Almost every evangelical Christian who goes to Jerusalem visits the site, which is known as Gordon's Calvary.[2]

When the Arabian prophet Muhammad (meaning "praised") began to bring his people to faith in one God (for whom the Arab word is "Allah") Jerusalem was his first *qiblah*, meaning the place toward which the Muslim worshiper faces when he prays. At that time, Muhammad and his followers were exiles from Mecca[3] and had no jurisdiction over its holy shrine, the Kaaba,[4] which later became the Muslim's *qiblah*. Jerusalem is now regarded as Islam's third holy city after Mecca, Muhammad's birthplace, and Medina, the site of his tomb, both in Arabia. Muslim tradition sanctifies the Dome of the Rock as the spot from which Muhammad, after a miraculous night journey from Mecca to Jerusalem, ascended through seven heavens to the throne of God and then descended back to earth.

The three great monotheistic faiths have another point in common. They recognize a common ancestor, Abraham. The Jews claim to be his physical children (John 8:33,53). The apostle Paul assures us that all true Christians are his spiritual seed (Gal. 3:29). Arab Muslims claim direct descent through his son Ishmael, whom God promised to make "a great nation" (Gen. 17:20). In a general sense, all believers—Jewish, Christian, and Muslim—claim kinship with Abraham, "the father of all them that believe" (Rom. 4:11).

From Bethlehem to Calvary, through Pentecost by way

of Samaria, Caesarea, Antioch, and on to Europe, Christianity was born and spread. Because faithful witnesses "turned the world upside down" (Acts 17:6), Christianity predominated in the lands of the Mediterranean basin by the end of the fifth century. But it gradually lost its New Testament purity and simplicity so that by the year A.D. 570, when Muhammad was born, the advocates of Christianity were more interested in splitting theological hairs over the person of Christ and the doctrine of the Trinity than in proclaiming the simple gospel of personal faith in the Christ of Calvary.

Muhammad's father died before the child's birth, and his mother before he reached the age of six. Reared by relatives, he hired out as a shepherd's helper as soon as he was old enough to tend a flock of sheep. Successively, he became camel driver, caravan leader, and husband of a wealthy Meccan widow whose business he had successfully promoted in Syria and Palestine.

Becoming financially independent through his marriage, Muhammad had time for meditation. His thoughts turned to his people and their pagan condition. Mecca, the religious capital of Arabia, was a center of animism and idolatry. Its shrine, the Kaaba, housed a different god for each day of the Arabic year (360).

Grieved by the idolatry, debauchery, and gambling of his fellow citizens, Muhammad began to spend long hours in meditation in a cave three miles from Mecca. Influenced by the one-God concept of Judaism and thrilled by the story of Jesus, he became convinced that what the Arabians needed was an inspired prophet who would lead them to faith in one God. Through visions and trances, daydreams and the encouragement of a doting wife, he came to the unshakable conviction that he was that prophet—that God had given him a message for his people. After winning a few supporters from among his immediate family, he went to the Kaaba and there, trembling with excitement, proclaimed in the very stronghold of pagan worship, "There is no god but God, and Muhammad is the apostle of God."

Muhammad's public declaration of faith in one God, his preaching of future judgment, and his denunciation of idolatry and other pagan practices won few followers in his native city, though he continued there for twelve years. At the age of fifty-two he was forced to flee to the city later known as Medina, 210 miles north of Mecca. The year of his flight marks the beginning of Muslim history. At Medina he set up the rule of Allah (God) with himself as dictator. Determined to abolish idolatry and to subdue both Judaism and Christianity to a role of dependence, he became the spiritual and political ruler of all Arabia before his death ten years later.

Before he died Muhammad sent envoys to the rulers of Greece, Persia, Egypt, Abyssinia, and even to the Byzantine emperor, commanding their acceptance of Islam. Confidently, he envisioned "mankind entering the religion of Allah in troops" (Koran 110:2). His vision was realized at least in part. Within a hundred years after his death the Muslim faith had spread from his native Arabia northward to Syria, westward to Egypt, Libya, Tunisia, Algeria, Morocco, and Spain, and eastward to Persia, India, and China.

Christianity lost a golden opportunity to enlist this zealous, reforming visionary from Arabia. As a traveling businessman, Muhammad had many contacts with Christianity. Wherein did the Christian witness of the seventh century fail? A noted Islamic scholar, Sir William Muir, declares: "Instead of the simple majesty of the gospel as a revelation of God reconciling mankind to Himself through His Son, the sacred dogma of the Trinity was forced upon the traveler . . . , and the worship of Mary was exhibited in so gross a form as to leave upon the mind of Muhammad the impression that she was held to be a god, if not the third person and the consort of the Deity."[5]

To the shame of seventh-century Christianity, this was the corrupt and superstitious form of the gospel with which Muhammad came in contact.

Theologically, the stricter monotheism of Judaism and Islam provide a more common doctrinal ground than obtains between Christianity and either of them. Politically and nationally, however, Muslims and Christians in the Middle East are closer together than either group is to the Jews. The tragedy of a divided Palestine, the issue of extreme Zionism, and the threat of an expanding Pan-Arabism are factors in a complicated situation that makes any attempt at a gospel witness in Arab lands a frustrating experience. No rapport is possible between Jews and Muslims; little rapport exists between Muslims and Christians. Evangelical Christians, especially, bear the stigma of a western orientation and origin, and the West is held to be pro-Jewish and, therefore, anti-Arab.

Yet, in the midst of this confusion the persistent question of the apostle Paul refuses to be silenced: "How shall they hear" (Rom. 10:14)—both Jew and Arab? Where does our responsibility lie? Every fresh generation of Christian believers is responsible for witnessing to the truth of the gospel to the whole world of its day. One seventh of our world today is Muslim. Some one hundred million of these worshipers are the Arabic-speaking sons of Ishmael, living in the Middle East in the area known as the Arab world, which stretches from the Persian Gulf westward to Casablanca on the Atlantic coast. Like Mount Everest to intrepid mountaineers before its conquest, the Arab world today presents to the followers of Christ their greatest unmet challenge.

Notes

[1] Islam, meaning "surrender," is the faith of Muslims collectively.

[2] General Gordon, first British High Commissioner in Palestine, discovered this site purported to be Golgotha, or Calvary. Nearby is a rock-hewn tomb, which could have been the one in which the body of Christ was laid.

[3] Mecca, the birthplace of Muhammad, is the city to which yearly pilgrimages are made by his followers.

[4] The Kaaba (meaning "cube"), the most venerated sanctuary of Islam, is situated in the center of the Great Mosque in Mecca. The approximately 35-foot cube contains the "Black Stone," which is kissed by all pilgrims to Mecca as an essential part of the ritual.

[5] Quoted by Canon Sell, *The Life of Muhammad* (London: The Christian Literature Society for India, 1913), pp. 15-16.

1
Problems For Those Who Hear

The sons of Ishmael face a multitude of problems as they hear and consider the message of the gospel. Brought up on the simple Muslim creed, "There is no God but God and Muhammad is the apostle [messenger] of God," they are thoroughly shaken when asked to reckon with the possibility that their traditional faith may not be *the* way to God, that the message of someone other than Muhammad must be taken into account, that there is one who claims unequivocally, "I am the truth."

A Muslim Student

In high school in his home city of Beirut, Lebanon, Abdullah[1] was asking embarrassing questions about Islam, the faith of his fathers. His inquiring mind had landed him in trouble with his teacher of religion before.

Although he was from the Sunni (traditional) sect of Muslims, Abdullah had secretly read parts of the New Testament. It was only natural for him to compare the teachings of Jesus in the Sermon on the Mount with what he had been taught from the Koran.[2]

When his teacher quoted the Koran on retaliation, "And one who attacketh you, attack him in like manner as he attacked you" (Koran 2:194), a statement of Jesus immediately came to Abdullah's mind, "But whosoever shall smite thee on thy right cheek, turn to him the other also" (Matthew 5:39).

"Which is right," he asked his teacher, "the Koran or the Gospel?"

"The Koran, of course," replied the teacher.

"But," persisted Abdullah, "does not the Koran exhort us to respect the Gospels as Scriptures revealed from God?" (Koran 5:66)

"The Gospels have been corrupted," retorted his teacher, voicing a timeworn cliché that Muslim teachers often used to refute the argument of Christian scholars.

The answer did not satisfy Abdullah. At the earliest opportunity he took up his copy of the New Testament to read it in secret again.

Graduation from high school found him wondering what he should do next. He had thought of some branch of engineering as a career. But where would he study?

"Let's go to the United States," a friend suggested.

A list of colleges was obtained from the United States Embassy in Beirut, letters were written, a visa was applied for, necessary affidavits were obtained, and Abdullah was eventually on his way. He enrolled in a college in one of the southern states and was soon contacted by a Baptist Student Union secretary who invited him to a social, then to a Bible-study group, and later to a Sunday service in a nearby Baptist church.

Abdullah enjoyed the singing of the choir, participated hesitantly in the congregational singing, listened eagerly to the preaching, and felt the warmth and kindness of church members. When he saw others walk down the church aisle one day in response to a gospel appeal, he, too, arose from his seat and went forward. He was not sure why he did so, but believed something was there that he ought to investigate, something that would lead him closer to the truth about God which, in his innermost being, he longed to discover.

Perhaps there was not time enough between the second and third stanzas of the invitation hymn for the sincere Baptist pastor to explain clearly to Abdullah what deciding for Christ means. Perhaps Abdullah's affirmative response to the pastor's leading question, "You do wish to accept Christ as your Saviour, don't you?" came too easily. Within a week he was baptized and his name placed on the membership roll of a Baptist church.

Abdullah worked part-time to help cover his college expenses, but he was soon in financial difficulties. Word leaked back to his family that he had become a Christian. He received warning letters and, when he ignored them, the financial aid he had been receiving from home was cut off. Deciding that full-time employment was the best way to provide a livelihood, he discontinued his studies.

Federal inspectors began to investigate this foreign student who, no longer enrolled in college, was engaged in full-time employment without a work permit. Abdullah became discouraged. Was this what becoming a Christian had brought him to? He was too proud and independent to ask Baptist friends for financial help. His attendance at church became spasmodic. Finally, he was deported back to Beirut at the expense of the United States Government.

Concealing the fact that he had become a Christian, Abdullah seized the opportunity to continue his education at a college in Cairo, Egypt. His troubles followed him to that Muslim country. A student who had been with him in the United States recognized him and reported to the college administration that Abdullah, having joined a Baptist church in America, was an infidel. Every attempt was made to bring Abdullah back to the fold of Islam—persuasion, threat of physical harm, warning of expulsion.

He returned to Beirut, but his reputation followed him. His home would not accept him. A cousin to whom he had become engaged would no longer consider him for marriage. Missionaries and Lebanese Baptists counseled with him and provided him with a room and some money for food until he was able to obtain a student visa and return to the States. Disillusioned because of white student reaction in Mississippi to his dark color, he left college again, sought work in New York, and was once more deported to Lebanon. Obtaining employment in Libya, he worked there for a brief period, after which he emigrated to Canada.

Not really sure what to believe, disillusioned with Islam, torn between family ties and loyalty to Christ, Abdullah's testimony as a Muslim convert to Christianity has been lost to his own people and his native land where it is most needed.

A Teen-age Muslim Girl

Fatimah, a Muslim teen-ager, is from the Shiite (meaning "splinter") sect. An intelligent and dilligent student in the Beirut (Lebanon) Baptist High School, she has so excelled in her studies that she has been granted a scholarship without which she could not continue in school. Listening to daily Bible lessons from dedicated teachers, attending school chapel five days a week, and observing the kindness of Baptist missionaries to her family, especially in their bereavement when her oldest brother died tragically at the age of fourteen, Fatimah became attracted to the Christian way of living. She has acknowledged Christ as her personal Saviour. Faithfully, she attends weekly meetings of the Young Woman's Auxiliary, enters wholeheartedly into the fellowship, participates in the program, and gives every evidence of having had an experience of saving grace.

Yet, Fatimah has little prospect of being baptized and taking her place publicly as a member of the Christian community. She is already of marriageable age. Before long, a marriage will be arranged for her with some man from her own sect, not in sympathy with her Christian convictions. No doubt she will instil something of the spirit of Christ into the lives of her children, but her testimony as a convert to Christianity will be largely lost as far as its practical effect upon her Shiite Muslim community is concerned. While cherishing her happy experiences as a student in the Baptist school, and perhaps remaining a Christian at heart, she will be tempted to follow the cultural pattern of her community and live ostensibly as a nominal Muslim.

A Druse Girl

Farhani's experience is happily different. A transfer student from a French school to the Beirut Baptist High School for her junior year, she came from an outstanding family of Druses, a heretical Muslim sect. Fluent in Arabic, French, and English, she made friends readily and fitted easily into the environment of a mission school. This was her first vital contact with evangelical Christianity.

During her first year at the Baptist school, one missionary taught her Bible and another taught her English.

Both remember her as quiet, attentive, and eager to absorb all that was presented of the Christian faith. She opened her heart to Christ and longed for the day when she could confess him publicly in baptism. In her senior year, she attended the services of the English-speaking University Baptist Church where she was a member of a Sunday School class taught by the wife[3] of a visiting professor who was serving at the Arab Baptist Theological Seminary near Beirut. Patiently, lovingly, the kind Sunday School teacher led her into a deeper, fuller appreciation of the Christian way of life.

Later, an opportunity came for Farhani to be baptized in the Jordan River at the traditional spot of Christ's own baptism. There, without her parents' knowledge, she made a public profession of her faith in Christ. In school-chapel services and church gatherings she has frequently given a public testimony of her Christian experience. Genuine concern for the salvation of her parents has led her to invite missionaries to her home to testify to them.

After graduation, Farhani worked for several years as a secretary and then came back to the Baptist High School to teach typing and French. In her own quiet way, she has helped greatly in witnessing to other students from non-Christian backgrounds.

Farhani's faith has been tried as her parents have attempted to arrange a marriage for her. She gave different reasons for rejecting successive suitors. One was too short, she said, another not well enough educated, still another too ugly, and another too fat. But one day she had no plausible reason for refusing a suitor who presented himself. A member of the Lebanese diplomatic corps, he was apparently all that a young woman could desire in a husband—youthful, handsome, wealthy, educated. What could Farhani tell her eager parents? For her, the suitor lacked one essential: He was not a believing Christian. She could have no real fellowship with him. After telling her parents she could not marry him because "I do not love him," she made her way to school with a heavy heart. She asked her missionary confidant to pray with her that her parents would not try to force her into marriage. God answered their prayer. Her parents did not press the issue.

She has now fallen genuinely in love with a fellow teacher at the Baptist high school. He is a handsome, intelligent, devout Christian. Together, with fear and trembling, they revealed to her parents their desire for marriage. Farhani's father has always shown a moderate spirit in religious matters. Her mother has been more insistent that she marry someone from their own faith, but the kindly attitude of the handsome Christian suitor has, little by little, won her heart. She has confided to her daugher that she thinks he is going to be her favorite son-in-law.

Reasonable parents, prayer, her own charming personality, and her genuine love for her family have helped to make Farhani's stand for Christ easier than is the lot of other converts from non-Christian backgrounds. Her desire is to help establish a genuine Christian home.[4] Is there a danger that she will become so completely absorbed into the Christian community that contact with her own Druse people will be weakened?

Farhani has always sought to live without compromising her Christian testimony. Her own family ties will remain, but she, in a sense, will be lifted out of a non-Christian community where her outstanding witness is needed so much. The strength of her testimony to her own people will depend largely on her degree of identification with them.

A Faithful Witness

No one in the Musaitbi Baptist Church of Beirut doubted the reality of Mahmoud's experience of salvation. This is how he came to know Christ.

Working as a polisher in a furniture factory, he had opportunity to evaluate Christianity as evidenced in the words and deeds of his workmate, Kisshaya, a young man from a Greek Catholic background. Mahmoud was not greatly impressed with what he saw and heard, but he liked Kisshaya as a friend who was easy to get along with and quite industrious. They sought for thrills in life, as most young men do, but they were not irreligious. In fact, both performed their outward religious duties with some degree of regularity.

Mahmoud was careful to observe Muslim feast days. He attended Friday prayers at the mosque and scrupulously participated in Ramadan, the Muslim month of fasting. At school he had memorized whole chapters of the Koran and could recite them easily.

Kisshaya had gone to a Greek Catholic school for several years. He was well acquainted with the formal ceremonies of the Greek Catholic Church, but his religion meant little to him. Regular attendance at confession had been a part of the school schedule. Often when asked by his father confessor to enumerate his sins so that he might be assigned the appropriate penance, Kisshaya would rack his brain and present an imaginary list of misdeeds that he had neither committed nor intended to commit.

Spiritually, there was little difference between Mahmoud and Kisshaya. They had been born into different religious communities, but neither knew the meaning of a vital experience with a personal God. They carried different identity cards,[5] one proclaiming Mahmoud a Sunni Muslim by religious affiliation, the other indicating that Kisshaya was a Christian of the Greek Catholic denomination; but both were sinners in need of a Saviour. When Mahmoud happened to scrape his knuckles on the workbench, he would vent his exasperation by cursing the owner of the factory and his fellow workers in the name of the Prophet Muhammad. Kisshaya would respond in like fashion, the difference being that the names of Catholic saints came more readily from his lips.

As Mahmoud and Kisshaya were thrown together in their daily task of lacquering furniture, a friendship of sorts developed. They began to spend their leisure time together, especially on payday evenings when they would seek entertainment in places of ill repute.

One Monday, Kisshaya was unusually quiet when he reported for work. Mahmoud inquired about his health.

"Don't you feel well?" he asked.

"Oh, I'm all right," answered Kisshaya.

As the week passed, Mahmoud wondered what had happened to his friend. He could see a definite change in him. There was no more foul language. Obscene stories no longer drew laughter from him.

"I'll see you as usual at eight o'clock at the same place," Mahmoud remarked on Friday after they had collected their pay packets.

This was standard practice for them. Friday was their big night.

To Mahmoud's surprise, Kisshaya replied, "I will not be going with you tonight."

"Why?" asked Mahmoud. "Do you have another appointment?"

"Yes," replied his friend. "I'm going to a prayer meeting at the Baptist church.

Mahmoud laughed and cursed his friend good-naturedly. "Don't tell me that you've got religion," he said.

Quietly, Kisshaya told him that on the previous Sunday he had accepted Christ as his Saviour and would, from that time on, try to live in accordance with the teachings of the New Testament. He explained that the conversion of his cousin, formerly an ardent Communist, through the testimony of a Baptist layman had created a stir and that he had gone to find out what could bring such a remarkable change in the life of one who had been an avowed atheist. The simple testimony of that Baptist, who was neither priest nor minister, had convinced him, also, he said, that there is more in Christianity than rite and ceremony.

Mahmoud was sure his friend's experience was just a passing phase, that in a few days he would be his usual self. But as weeks and months passed, the quiet, consistent testimony of Kisshaya convinced him that the change was permanent. The emptiness of his own life, the lack of real joy, led him to ask questions. He felt that it would be impossible for him ever to become a Christian. He was born a Muslim and expected to die a Muslim. But Kisshaya began to pray for him and gave him a copy of the New Testament, which Mahmoud promised to read.

Occasionally during the next two years Mahmoud

accepted Kisshaya's invitation to attend a Baptist service, a prayer meeting, or a Bible study class. He came in contact there with people who radiated happiness and contentment. God's Holy Spirit began working in Mahmoud's heart, convicting him of sin and convincing him of his need of a Saviour. One day he went to see a missionary who was working with the Baptist church. Mahmoud expressed to the missionary his desire to become a Christian like his friend Kisshaya.

Thrilled with the opportunity to explain more fully the plan of salvation and the meaning of the Christian life, the missionary opened the New Testament and had Mahmoud read verses that pointed to the truths he had already seen exemplified in the life of his friend. As they bowed together in prayer, the Holy Spirit completed his work of grace in the young Muslim's heart.

In due time, Mahmoud was baptized. Like many of the other converts in the Middle East, he has problems. Persecution from his family is more subtle than physical, however. Being the oldest son in the family, he is the main breadwinner in his home, for his father is too old to work. Mahmoud's faithfulness in providing a livelihood for the family has helped to temper the persecution that he has inevitably suffered. Because his help in the home is indispensable, he has not been cast out.

Mahmoud's main problem is marriage. His father complains daily because he refuses to marry one of his Muslim cousins, and Mahmoud has determined to marry no one who is not a born-again Christian. No sincere Muslim father will give his daughter to an "infidel Christian," and Christian parents hesitate to give a daughter to a Muslim convert because they have known Muslim converts who have backslidden. Then, too, in the Arab world a bride usually comes under the influence and care of her mother-in-law, and the mother-in-law's treatment of her daughter-in-law is proverbially harsh. Perhaps Mahmoud will never marry. Someday he may be tempted to marry a Muslim girl and, in doing so, compromise his own Christian testimony. He still lives with his family. At least, this contact provides a daily witness for Christ in a Muslim community.

Is It Worthwhile?

These situations, all of them from Lebanon, illustrate some of the problems associated with the Christian witness in the Arab world. Lebanon permits religious freedom. Officially, it is possible there to change one's religion. In Syria, Jordan, Egypt, Libya, and Yemen, however, proselytizing Muslims is forbidden by law. Persecution is fierce in those areas, and no convert's life is safe.

Considering these problems, is it worthwhile to continue a Christian witness to Muslims? Is continued expenditure of Southern Baptist resources for mission work in the Arab world justified? These questions are asked by sincere supporters of missions who rightly expect the best return possible from their investment in the missionary cause.

There is only one proper answer. The last earthly command of the highest authority, the Lord Jesus Christ, impels Southern Baptist missionaries to witness to the whole wide world, of which the Arab section remains one of the most challenging areas. In the words of Dr. Billy Graham at the World Congress on Evangelism in Berlin (1966), "The primary task of the church is the penetration of the whole world with the gospel."[6] The

Muslim world, with the Arab world as its hard core, has largely withstood the efforts of courageous missionaries from various Christian groups. But the command of Jesus to go, backed with his unfailing promise to accompany those who dare to obey, inspires some of his followers today to take the risk, believing that what seems humanly impossible may become possible by God's power.

The Christian's marching orders are given explicitly in the Great Commission. It is not for him to surrender, or retreat, or become discouraged because of unfavorable circumstances or meager results. His task is to confront the people of the Arab world with the claims of Jesus Christ. These claims are being considered by many of the sons of Ishmael today as they hear the message of the Cross proclaimed by faithful witnesses.

Notes

[1] In order to avoid reprisal, fictitious names are sometimes substituted for real names of nationals throughout this book.

[2] Koran means "reading." The book contains 114 chapters (*surahs*) which, except for the brief opening chapter, are arranged in order of length. Muslims claim that the Koran is an exact copy of the original in heaven given by revelation to Muhammad, through the medium of the angel Gabriel.

[3] Mrs. J. Wash Watts who, with her husband, dean emeritus of New Orleans Baptist Theological Seminary, taught at the seminary in Beirut during its second year of operation.

[4] Farhani was married in a Christian ceremony on September 1, 1967.

[5] Personal identity cards, issued at the time of birth registration, list, among other vital statistics, the religious persuasion into which a child is born.

[6] Billy Graham, "Stains on the Altar," *One Race, One Gospel, One Task* (Minneapolis: World Wide Publications, 1967), I, 152.

2
Who Must Hear

"Arabs" are listed among the peoples represented in the apostle Peter's congregation on the day of Pentecost. No doubt they were mentioned because of their dis-tinctive language as well as for the nation or country from which they had come. Who are the Arabs today?

The Arabs—One People or Many?

In its truest sense, the term "Arab" applies only to the native Semitic tribes of Arabia. Many non-Arabians call themselves Arabs, however. Their claim is justified if considered in relation to traits and social attitudes held in common by nearly a hundred million people living in countries of the Fertile Crescent,[1] the Arabian Peninsula, those African countries bounded on the north by the Mediterranean Sea, and in addition the northern regions of the Sudan and some of the new African states; also, minority groups of Arabs (looked at from the point of view of a basically common culture) are found in Israel, East Africa, the island of Madagascar, and as far east as Indonesia.

The cultural unity of the inhabitants of most of these countries has, over the centuries, depended largely on their geographical contiguity. Constant contacts of their peoples in trade and marriage have helped to spread Arabic culture.

A Common Language

One common language is a dominant unifying factor of Arabic culture. Classical Arabic, understood by all literate Arabs from the Persian Gulf to the Atlantic Ocean, is uniform, though local dialects are often mutually unintelligible. A modified classical Arabic, the language of mass media—press, radio, and films—has been developed as the common language. It is the vehicle of instruction in Arabic schools of higher learning and the acceptable language of the pulpit, whether Muslim or Christian.

Written from right to left in cursive characters, Arabic is based on three-letter roots from which the majority of its words are made by adding prefixes or suffixes. Westerners generally have difficulty in mastering the language because of its intricate grammatical structure and its guttural sounds, some of them peculiar to Semitic languages. Arabic has sounds which run from the lightest breath to the heaviest growl. It has all the consonants used in English with some more added (for example, a heavy T and a light T, a heavy S and a light S, with added variations under certain conditions). John Van Ess, attempting (in his book, *Meet the Arab,* published in 1943) to describe some of these sounds, talks about "a vigorous gargle, and a high-pressure puncture, and a strangling Q and a sort of vomitic gag which is the despair of the foreigner."

Arabic purists are unwilling to introduce foreign words into their vocabulary. They may be obliged to incorporate some foreign technological term into the language temporarily, but before long they find an exact Arabic equivalent based on one of the three-consonant roots in which they believe every germinal idea can be expressed. This insistence on keeping the Arabic language pure has contributed to the unity of Arabic culture.

Other languages, including English, have many words derived from Arabic. Common English words of Arabic origin (transmitted through the Spanish language) include: admiral, algebra, cipher, mattress, gazelle, coffee, sugar, alcohol, cotton, sherbet; also, such place-names as Gilbraltar and Guadalcanal, corrupted somewhat in transmission.

A *Predominant Religion*

Islam, the religion of 95 percent of all Arabs, is the greatest unifying force in the Arab world. Its strict legalistic codes regulate both the spiritual and the social life of individuals and communities. Islam is interpreted in relation to five "pillars" and six main tenets or articles of faith.

The five pillars of Islam are: Recital of the creed, five stated daily periods of prayer, payment of alms, fasting during the month of Ramadan, and a pilgrimage to Mecca.

Creed.—Simple repetition of the creed ("There is no god but God and Muhammad is the apostle of God") three times sincerely from the heart initiates one into the Muslim faith. During a visit to Baghdad in Iraq, the writer was refused entry into a Shiite mosque, although many mosques are open to tourists. "Repeat the creed," was the demand of the responsible sheikh,[2] "and you may enter."

Prayer.—The periods of prayer are: dawn to sunrise, commencing as soon as it is light enough to distinguish between a white thread and a black one; at high noon when the sun begins to decline; in the late afternoon when the sun is about to set; a few minutes after sunset; and when night has closed in. When using public transportation, some Muslims will insist that the vehicle in which they are traveling be halted in order that they may get out their prayer rugs and, after ceremonial ablutions, face in the direction of Mecca for their ritual of prayer.

Alms.—The Koran commands a religious tax. The amount of alms required is 2½ percent, or a fortieth of one's income. In addition to the "legal alms," voluntary offerings are also prescribed.

Fasting.—Ramadan, the tenth month of the lunar year, varies from year to year since the lunar year is shorter than the solar year by some ten days. Ramadan completes the Christian calendar every thirty-three years. During the month of daily fasting no food or drink may be partaken of from sunrise to sunset. Even the swallowing of saliva is forbidden. However, the night is spent in feasting to make up for the day's fast.

Pilgrimage.—The pilgrimage to Mecca, undertaken in the twelfth month of the Muslim year, is required once in a lifetime of every male Muslim who can pay his own expenses and provide for his family during his absence. Any woman who goes on this pilgrimage must be accompanied by her husband or a male relative. Zealous widows have been known to acquire husbands for the occasion, conveniently divorcing them on their return home. Since the pilgrimage annually brings together thousands of Muslims of every color, language, economic status, and nationality, it is a unifying symbol of Islam.

Islam's six articles of faith have to do with the unity of God, the angels, the inspired books, the inspired prophets, the decrees of God, and the day of judgment:

Unity of God.—God is one. He has no partner. The Christian doctrine of the Trinity is an abomination. The power of an unchanging God (Allah) makes him the author of all things whether they seem good or bad.

Angels.—There is a hierarchy of angelic, reasoning beings, created of light. Each individual human being has two recording angels to write down his good and evil deeds, respectively.

Inspired books.—Of the holy books inspired by God, the Koran is his latest revelation and supersedes all others. The Old and New Testaments of the Christian Bible were also given by God, but are corrupted in their present form.

Inspired prophets.—The six eminent prophets sent by God are Adam, the chosen of Allah; Noah, the preacher of Allah; Abraham, the friend of Allah; Moses, the spokesman of Allah; Jesus, the word of Allah; Muhammad, the apostle of Allah.

Decrees of God.—Everything that happens, whether good or bad, is foreordained by the unchangeable decrees of Allah. (The fatalism resulting from this doctrine is all too evident in the daily life of individuals throughout the world of Islam.)

Day of Judgment.—On the day of judgment the soul will cross a bridge of great length as slender as a hair and as sharp as a sword. Those who are evil will lose their balance and fall into the fires of hell below. The saved will, through the intercession of Muhammad, pass with the speed of light into paradise with its gardens of delight, affording luscious fruits, rivers of wine that does not intoxicate, and beautiful women for the pleasure of the faithful.

Despite the diversification of Islam into more than a hundred and fifty major and minor sects, Muslims are conscious of spiritual ties uniting them as believers in opposition to all unbelievers.

A Common Way of Life

A general common pattern of life prevails throughout the Arab world. Bedouin of the Arabian desert and nomads of the Sahara would feel at home in each other's company. Social and family customs and habits of courtesy vary only slightly in the widely separated cities of Baghdad, Damascus, and Cairo.

Hospitality.—Arabs are proverbially hospitable. For them, hospitality is a greater virtue than honesty, and a man will incur debt to avoid being inhospitable. On a visit in northern Jordan a missionary couple entered, without prior notice, the home of one of the chief men of the village. As noontime approached their host brought in a young goat to provide food for them. When the missionaries protested, he warned them, half jokingly, that if they declined the hospitality they would, according to Arabic custom, be obliged to pay the full value of the goat in addition to forfeiting their lunch. Among bedouin Arabs, hospitality is a means of expressing one's gratitude to God, "the Bountiful, the All-merciful," for the necessities of life.

Guests of high social standing who are accompanied by any sizable group of attendants may have a camel butchered in their honor, stuffed with as many sheep as its stomach will hold, with each sheep in turn stuffed with as many chickens as it can contain, and each chicken stuffed to capacity with eggs. This bountiful fare, starting with the camel's right eye presented to the honored guest, is served on a mountain of rice sodden with savory gravy. The guests and host dine first, followed by men of lesser rank. Women are way down in the eating order and usually get the scraps that are left. After a great show of hospitality towards guests of rank, bedouin Arabs often eat frugally for weeks. A common response to the question, "Have you eaten?" is "Yes, I ate two days ago," meaning that a hearty meal was eaten then and that the speaker has no need yet of a substantial meal.

Courtesy.—Arabs are meticulously courteous. When two meet, the one who is socially superior initiates a polite exchange of courteous greetings. The older of two bedouin usually places his hands upon his chest while the other bows deeply, reaching toward the ground with his right hand and then placing it on his forehead in token of respect. When two men of equal social rank meet, each kisses his hand and places it on the forehead of the other man. Village women show their deference to visiting female friends by excitedly welcoming them afresh every few minutes, especially if the conversation lags.

A most discourteous gesture is to sit facing someone with the soles of one's feet exposed directly in his line of vision. Dogs or pigs or other animals traditionally held in contempt must not be introduced or their names mentioned in the presence of guests. One Western diplomat made his presence offensive to Arab dignitaries when he thoughtlessly brought his favorite dog along to a public celebration. They requested his government to recall him because of his unpardonable breach of etiquette.

Reticence.—Arabs usually hesitate to reveal anything

about their personal lives. The reason may be rooted in primitive superstition. Even intelligent, well-informed Arabs sometimes refuse to disclose their private affairs for fear of being exposed to the evil eye of a malevolent spirit. Bedouin Arabs honor this fundamental principle of reticence in their guests. A stranger may spend three days enjoying the shelter, protection, and hospitality of a bedouin tent without any obligation to disclose his name, origin, destination, or the purpose of his visit.

Individualism.—A spirit of individualism is prominent among Arabs. The urge for private enterprise is more dominant than the necessity for cooperative action. Close relatives sometimes engage in business of the same kind in stores or offices on the same street, or even in adjacent buildings, rather than cooperate in a joint, consolidated, stronger venture. Desire for self-assertion is powerful and, linked with a love for individual freedom, often obscures the advantages of collective action.

Conformity.—Balancing the strong individualism of the Arab is his adherence to custom and tradition. One who steps out of the circle of time-honored practice or who introduces innovations is frowned on by the community. Any man who seeks a wife outside his traditional environment is sure to call down the wrath of his elders upon his head. Marriage is supposed to take place within the community. Inherited religious ties are sacred. Woe betide the one who breaks them! Having brought shame on himself, his family, and his society, he may be barred completely from his community. His action has testified more eloquently than words that he considers the religion of his fathers false and not good enough for him.

Resignation.—A calm resignation that is equivalent to fatalism characterizes most Arabs who live away from cosmopolitan cities. This stoic virtue is commendable in that it accepts misfortune without complaint; but it also encourages callousness toward human suffering and a do-nothing attitude that discourages progress. When the writer lived in a Jordanian village of five thousand inhabitants without an adequate water supply, he encouraged the village elders to have water pumped in from a source one mile from the town. The cost per household would have been less than five dollars. The only response was, "If God had willed that we should have other than rain [cistern] water for our needs, he would have provided it without our doing anything about it." Their philosophy is that whatever happens is ordained by God, should not be questioned, and must not be altered. To them, all circumstances, favorable and otherwise, are part of the predetermined, unchangeable plan of God for his creatures.

Procedure in Marriage

Marriage in the Arab world is a serious business. It is not entered into lightly. Conceived as a union of two families more than of two individuals, it is generally arranged by the respective parents. Tentative feelers are put out to see if there is any possibility of a marriage agreement. Face-saving is so important to the Arab that a parent would prefer to ask in a roundabout way for the hand of a suitable girl for his son, with the possibility of receiving an indirect no, rather than be faced with the embarrassment of a public refusal. Marriages are customarily arranged between families of equal social standing. The girl is consulted by her parents in the matter of the suitor of their choice. She may have the privilege of rejecting a suitor, but not of replacing him by someone of her own choice.

After the initial agreement, the father of the prospective bridegroom goes to the home of the bride to enter into more official transactions. A price must be paid, and a lengthy bargaining procedure takes place, involving the relative merits, qualities, economic status, and prestige of the two families. The prospective bride will be lost to her own family, but at the highest price they can gain for her. When ready cash is not available, the bridegroom may offer his own sister in exchange as a bride for the brother of the maiden he himself wishes to marry. Such an exchange may be desirable also because it would cement relations between the two families.

With the price agreed upon, a formal engagement ceremony is arranged. Relatives and friends are invited. A Muslim priest is present to invoke the blessing of God and read a portion of the Koran. (Or, if the family is Greek Orthodox or Roman Catholic, a Christian priest reads from the Bible or book of ritual.) After that, the engaged couple will have opportunities to become acquainted with each other, but always under the watchful eye of a chaperon until after the marriage ceremony. An engagement between Arabs is a binding transaction. If broken off, the disgrace to the girl is such that further possibility of marriage often is ended for her.

Traditionally, the prospective bride's cousin, the son of her father's brother, has first claim on her. A few years ago in Jordan, where Muslim customs have greatly influenced Christian communities, the hand of a pretty girl from a Catholic family was being sought by a young man from a well-to-do family in another village. The price was good, and a down payment was made, but before arrangements were completed the girl's cousin, who was from a poorer family, came home unexpectedly on leave from the army. When he learned of the situation he insisted on his prior right.

"I am her cousin," he declared, "and I wish to claim her for myself."

The chagrined father of the girl was obliged to call off the deal with the rich young suitor. Reluctantly, he sent back the first payment and told his daughter to wait until her cousin should be ready to marry her.

With marriage arranged within the family, the risk of divorce is slight. If romantic love is not present, family ties and affection are strong. So many people have been in on the arrangements that family pride is at stake, and everyone concerned does his utmost to make the union a lasting success. The bride goes to live with her husband's family. Families are consolidated by such unions. Blood ties are strengthened.

The entire family of brothers, sisters, uncles, aunts, and cousins, paternally and maternally related, feel a common bond of kinship that is a formidable force against any economic, social, or religious changes. To reach such a well-knit community for Christ is a difficult and challenging task.

Three Main Groups

Arabs may be classed in three groups: bedouin, *fellahin,* and *hadar,*[3] meaning, respectively, desert nomads, country people, and city dwellers.

Bedouin

Most picturesque and romantic of all the Arab peoples

are the "sons of the desert" known as bedouin. They take their name from a word (*badiyah*) that means desert or waste region. Their typical dwelling place is the vast expanse of sand dunes in the Arabian, Syrian, Iraqi, Jordanian, and North African deserts, although some live in the fertile central valley of Lebanon. These proud nomads spend the rainy winter months in the desert where sufficient grazing may be found temporarily for their livestock—sheep, goats, camels, donkeys, a few horses. They move in toward oases or rivers during the hot, dry summer. In Lebanon their annual migration is more vertical than horizontal, from the coastal plain or central valley in winter to the mountain slopes in summer. Most bedouin are herdsmen. Agricultural pursuits and all forms of industry are beneath their dignity.

The tribal system still prevails among all bedouin. A tribe may include as many as seven thousand tents or as few as forty. A single tent houses a man, his wife, and unmarried children. Around him will be the tents of his married sons, brothers, and male cousins.

The bedouin tent is part of the family property. As a rule it is made from black goat's hair. Tough and water repellant, the black tent material may be adorned with a white goat-hair stripe woven into it along the whole length of the tent walls. A curtain usually divides the tent into two rooms, one reserved for the head of the family and his guests and the other for the women, children, supplies of food, bedding, and a few essentials of household equipment with perhaps a corner reserved for a donkey or favorite horse.

All domestic duties fall to the bedouin women. They grind the wheat in the hand mill or pound it in the mortar. They knead and bake the bread, make butter and cheese, draw water from the well, weave cloth, and mend tents. When camp is struck they roll up the tents. One task is usually reserved for the men—the making of coffee. This is quite a ceremony, from the roasting and grinding of the coffee beans to the final serving in small cups. Boys at an early age are taught how to entertain guests with special emphasis on the serving of coffee. Making coffee and serving it are duties too important to be delegated to women, the bedouin think.

A bedouin woman enjoys little freedom. Before being weaned as a baby she is probably promised in marriage to a boy not yet concerned about finding a wife. In her unmarried state she recognizes the authority of her father, whose word is law in the bedouin family. Later she transfers her obedience to her husband, whose property she is by virtue of the price he has paid for her. Arab men boast of the amount they have paid for their wives, the price depending on the woman's looks, general health, and family status. A missionary was discussing this matter with some Arab acquaintances. Each in turn indicated the high cost of marriage.

Then they turned to the missionary and asked, "How much did you pay for your wife?"

"Nothing," he replied.

"We thought so," they said. She was somewhat plain and quite thin.

Bedouin object to the regimentation of any national government. Consequently, they are hard to control. Israel, Jordan, and Egypt have never been able to contain the bedouin within their domains. Tribes have spread-eagled across the borders of enemy countries, acknowledging allegiance to neither. The grazing area partitioned among the tribes by age-old traditional right is accepted by the bedouin as his. The question of ownership never enters his mind. Most governments wisely let bedouin go on their way with a minimum of interference.

A large tribe of bedouin will be composed of several groups of close relatives. Different tribes may in turn unite into confederations. Although the sheikh, the elected tribal head, has considerable power, his word is not in itself law. Before presenting his decision in any matter of importance he wisely counsels with his elders, who are the elected representatives of their families. The decision is thus accepted as the collective opinion of the tribe as represented in its duly elected elders.

Tribal loyalty is strong among bedouin Arabs. Their individualism prevents any general feeling of loyalty to a nation, but the sharing of traditions and hardships draws them into close relationships on a tribal level. Also, their blood ties constitute an unbreakable bond. A bedouin would rather die than endure the shame of being expelled from his tribe. A man without a tribe in the desert is suspect. People feel that he must be a renegade from justice.

This tribal loyalty may seem to be a barrier in spreading the kingdom of Christ among the Arab peoples, but it could be a great asset. Some years ago an Arab Christian presented the gospel to a seminomad bedouin tribe in the area of Baalbek, Lebanon, near the Syrian border. The tribal chief was kind and considerate when he understood that no political strings were attached to the ministry of the preacher.

When the sheikh's wife died, he was concerned about the care needed by his son and heir. He sent the boy,

Talal Sheiban, to be cared for in the Near East Home for Boys, administered by American evangelical missionaries in a mountain village about eight miles from the city of Beirut. The kindness of the missionaries won the heart of the old sheikh, and Talal grew up in a genuine Christian atmosphere. Through simple Bible teaching, a daily orphanage worship program, and counseling, the missionaries patiently led Talal to the point of decision. One day he knelt with his missionary foster father and prayed, "Lord Jesus, come into my heart, cleanse me from sin, make me thine." He was later baptized.

During the summer seasons Talal would return to his tribal encampment. A strong bond of affection existed between him and his father. The boy would tell of his experiences, how the boys in the home studied English, sang, attended daily prayers, and learned about a Heavenly Father who sent his Son to bring sinful, wandering mankind back to God. The father began to study the Bible and it was not long before he, too, made a profession of faith in Christ. Since he was the beloved and respected head of his tribe, his stand for Christ was not met with violent opposition. He has since died and Talal is recognized as his successor.

Talal's contact with city life has led him to believe that his people need to be educated as a means of bringing them to the true knowledge of God. He has opened a school for the young people of his encampment. The Bible is taught there as a part of the daily program. Talal is married to a girl from his own people. He has thus preserved his contact with them. As their leader, he is one of them. Not all of his people have accepted his new way of life. He realizes that faith in Christ for them will be an individual experience as it was for him. Tribal loyalty has kept the Sheiban clan together even with their leader professing Christ.

Villagers

Fellahin live in villages of various sizes and cultivate the surrounding land or engage in small businesses. These village merchants serve as a link with the outside world, bringing in the products of modern industry and exchanging them for the crops of the land.

Although some village families are more prosperous than others, there is little evidence of class distinction among them. Usually, the headman is elected from one of the most prosperous families. In some Arab countries these leaders now receive cash payment for their services, but in others their payment is still some livestock and a set quantity of wheat from each household. This elected office is sought because of the social prestige it affords and for the indirect political and economic benefits that come from contact with officialdom.

Maintaining public order, settling disputes, and preserving a link with regional and central governments are the headman's main responsibilities. His signature is registered with the government, and he carries a seal with which he stamps all official documents. Missionaries who cultivate the friendship of these officials find that their sympathetic attitude can pave the way for the gospel witness to enter their villages.

Village life varies from country to country in the Arab world. Structurally, variations depend on the climate and the building materials available. Sloping tiled roofs are necessary for protection from the winter snows in the mountains of Lebanon. In Egypt and other North African countries where stones are scarce, the walls of houses are usually made of dried clay bricks, and their flat roofs are constructed from a compound of mud and leaves laid over bamboo slats.

Dwellings, shops, and public buildings in flat country are usually concentrated in the center of the village, with cultivated plots radiating outward. In contrast, Lebanon's mountain villages occupy prominent heights with crop-bearing fields, fruit orchards, and olive groves often some distance away in the valleys below. In the larger villages, related families tend to live in a particular section and cultivate adjacent plots of ground.

Where more than one religious faith is represented in a village, people of the same faith will live in the same area, their dwellings built close to their house of worship. Consequently, traditional religious barriers are strong. Religious identity is zealously guarded.

City Dwellers

Throughout the Middle East, city life exercises a predominant influence. The two cities that challenge each other for the title of oldest continuously inhabited city are Damascus, the capital of Syria, and Aleppo, until recently its most populous center. The three great monotheistic religions born in this area have extended their influence from great city centers. The disciples of Jesus were first called Christians in the city of Antioch (Acts 11:26), which was then a part of Syria, and from there Christianity spread with amazing rapidity throughout the Roman Empire. When the cities of Mecca and Medina acknowledged the authority of Muhammad, he felt that his cause had succeeded; one city after another fell to his marching armies, and Islam became a world religion. For years the Passover ritual of the Jews has included the meaningful phrase, "Next year in Jerusalem," indicating the importance of that city in Jewish life.

In larger cities, as in villages, people tend to live in groups defined by nationality, religion, and occupation. Until twenty years ago the Old City of Jerusalem had its well-defined Jewish quarter, its Muslim quarter, and its different Christian quarters—Armenian, Catholic, Orthodox. The vast majority of the more than half a million people in the Shubra area of Cairo are Coptic Christians. Beirut, Lebanon, has its Muslim areas, its sections for Christians, and its Druse locality. Newer residential areas in large cities, however, tend to break down religious distinctions, with population distribution on the basis of socal and economic strata.

The traditional Arab town in Muslim countries still unites around the mosque, which serves as a community center as well as a religious focus. Religion is not the sole topic of conversation in the vicinity of the mosque. Politics, life, and religion are so closely linked for Muslims that the Friday sermon is often a vehicle for political propaganda on an international level. Some people look on Islam as a state religion. It could be described just as accurately as a religious state.

Small tradesmen of similar occupations tend to operate in the same quarter—a legacy of the guild system handed down from the medieval period. A city will have its street of blacksmiths, its carpenters' quarters, its jewelers' section, its confectioners' locality, and its piece-goods market. Although convenient for the shopper who wants to compare prices and quality and to bargain for a particular item of merchandise, this has the disadvantage of necessitating visits to several areas of town to complete his shopping list. Single stores that sell all kinds of consumer goods are comparatively new in the Arab world. A few department and variety stores, organized by enterprising Western-oriented businessmen, have sprung up in the larger cities.

Population Shift

Few bedouin ever become villagers, but many villagers move to the cities for economic, educational, and vocational reasons. Away from the influences of their traditional environment and caught up in a more cosmopolitan society, they are freer to absorb new ideas and even to change their religious affiliation.

Present-day missionary strategy resembles that of the early apostolic churches. Like Paul, most missionaries today concentrate their witness on the areas of dense population. Cities of the Arab world are teeming with people. Strong indigenous churches must be established in the population centers. These in turn must reach out to the country towns and villages. Representatives of the villages are living now in metropolitan centers. They return to their village communities at various seasons of the year—for a summer vacation, for the purpose of voting, to celebrate religious festivals, to show off a newborn child to proud grandparents, on the occasion of funerals, and for the celebration of marriages. If won to Christ, these rural transfers to the city constitute living links for the spread of the gospel across the land.

Nomads of the desert, villagers, city dwellers! Concerning them, the question keeps ringing: "How shall they hear?"

Notes

[1] "Fertile Crescent" is a term used to denote the band of arable land forming an arc around the northern part of the Syrian desert, flanked on the west and east by the basins of the Nile and the Euphrates-Tigris rivers, and arching into Israel, Jordan, Lebanon, and Syria.

[2] Muslim priest or preacher in the mosque.

[3] Bedouin (the word is both singular and plural) denotes a desert nomad generally. *Fellahin,* meaning plowmen or peasants, comes from a verb meaning "to cleave the soil." *Hadar* means "civilized."

3
Hearing
Through Travel

The modern Baptist witness in the Arab world commenced in the country of Lebanon in the last decade of the nineteenth century, and the way it began is unusual. Marvelous are God's ways for fulfilling his redemptive purposes for mankind!

Baptists in Lebanon

Something of the wanderlust of the ancient Phoenicians still flows in the bloodstream of the Lebanese who live today in part of the area known two thousand years before Christ as Phoenicia. The urge to travel caused a young Lebanese photographer named Said Jureidini[1] to seize the opportunity to accompany his uncle as part of the personnel with the Turkish exhibit to the 1893 Chicago World's Fair. Said's uncle demonstrated the antics of a camel before which animal Said danced, sword in hand, in the oriental fashion typical of Arabs.

No doubt, Said saw in Chicago many new and wonderful sights. He may have listened there on the fairgrounds to the preaching of men like Dwight L. Moody and Thomas Spurgeon, son of the famous Charles H. Spurgeon. At any rate, in his heart was a spiritual hunger he could neither understand nor satisfy. Said was a nominal Christian, a member of the Greek Orthodox Church, but he had no vital personal relationship with God.

Accepting an invitation from a friend in St. Louis, Missouri, Said visited that city and while there attended the Third Baptist Church, of which W. R. L. Smith was pastor. A revival meeting was in progress, and Said was present night after night. As the invitation hymn was being sung at the close of one memorable service, Dr. Smith observed in the audience a young man so deeply moved that tears were welling up in his eyes. Leaving the rostrum, the pastor went to where the young man, Said, was standing, laid his hand on his shoulder, and requested the privilage of helping him.

"Oh, my sins!" cried Said. "They are as an unbearable burden on my back. Who can help me get deliverance from them?"

As they talked together, Dr. Smith had the joy of pointing Said to Christ, the sin-bearer, whom the young man from Lebanon accepted in simple faith as his Saviour.

Thus it was that Said Jureidini left his homeland, traveled to Chicago, Illinois, found Christ as his Saviour in St. Louis, Missouri, and then, after a few months, returned to his native land to resume his work as a photographer and watch-repairer. So full was his heart with the joy of the Lord that he urged all his customers and friends to accept his Saviour as their own.

Gathering friends and relatives for Bible-study and prayer, Said soon found himself leader of a considerable number of converts. Not knowing what to do next, he wrote to his friend, Dr. Smith, for advice. A reply came stating that Dr. Smith and a group of Baptist friends were planning to visit the Middle East soon. They would come to Beirut to examine and baptize the new converts with a view to establishing the first modern Baptist church in Bible lands. Dr. Smith duly arrived, instructed and baptized Said's converts, and guided them in the organization of the church. Before the visitors moved on to Jerusalem, the new church asked that Said Jureidini be ordained to the gospel ministry as the first Arabic-speaking Baptist pastor.

Another young man, Daoud Yusuf from the town of Richaya el Wadi on the western slope of Mount Hermon, traveled to America at the turn of the century. He found Christ as his Saviour in Dallas, Texas, at the First Baptist church through the ministry of George W. Truett. Returning to Lebanon with the promise of some financial support from Baptists in southern Illinois, Daoud opened a school in his native town and later extended the Baptist witness to the nearby village of Kefr Mishky.

Baptists of the world, who had organized into the fellowship of the Baptist World Alliance in 1905, met in 1920 in a historic London conference, during which Baptist groups of different nations accepted responsibility for missionary work in various parts of the world. Southern Baptists were given the privilege of promoting a Baptist witness in the area traditionally known as the Bible Lands.

In 1923 the Foreign Mission Board of the Southern Baptist Convention sent out missionaries who took up residence in Jerusalem. Fred and Ruth Pearson and J. Wash and Mattie Watts were the first to form the Near East Baptist Mission. Part of Dr. Watts's ministry was to visit the Baptist work in Lebanon periodically. In 1927 the Southern Baptist board accepted financial responsibility for the work in Lebanon.

Tragedies struck the families of the pioneer missionaries: Sickness forced their return to the United States. Other missionaries were sent, but for various reasons—health, the outbreak of World War II in 1939, or family circumstances—their service was limited to one or two terms. All of the earlier missionaries lived in the area then called Palestine and made periodic visits to Lebanon to counsel with the Lebanese Baptist leaders who welcomed these friends.

In 1945 three missionary couples—Merrel and Beth Callaway, Henry and Julia Hagood, and Robert and Margaret Lindsey—arrived in Jerusalem. The Callaways lived in Beirut for a few months, but moved to Jerusalem, then later to Bahrein on the Persian Gulf for language study. The Hagoods lived in Nazareth, while the Lindseys remained in Jerusalem.

Tragedy again struck the little group of missionaries. Henry Hagood became ill and died suddenly, leaving his widow with one small son, Jimmie. The missionary was buried on the shores of Lake Galilee.

A young Baptist from Scotland, Finlay Graham, whose service as a British Royal Air Force flyer had brought him to Jerusalem during World War II, became burdened with the spiritual needs of the Arab world. Returning to Jerusalem in 1946, he began the study of Arabic and came into contact with Southern Baptist missionaries, among them the widowed Julia Saccar Hagood who became his wife on September 11, 1947, the same day that he was formally appointed a missionary by the Southern Baptist Foreign Mission Board. A very happy man—this new missionary!

Leaving her ministry in the George W. Truett Baptist

Orphanage—then in Nazareth—Julia Graham accompanied her husband to the village of Taiybeh in Jordan where they served eight months. During that time Missionary Graham made periodic visits to Beirut, Lebanon, to disburse funds allocated by the Foreign Mission Board. Each visit brought a deepening conviction that a missionary should live there to counsel with Lebanese nationals on the promotion of the Baptist witness in that country. After much prayer, the Grahams left Jordan and took up residence in Beirut in November of 1948. This move inaugurated a new phase of Baptist growth in Lebanon.

One small but active congregation in Beirut and a smaller struggling church in Kefr Mishky comprised the Baptist constituency in Lebanon in 1948. But nationals and missionaries witnessed, worked, and prayed, and God opened doors.

The outreach of the Beirut Baptist Church soon resulted in the organization of new work in Tripoli in the north, Mieh-Mieh in the south, and Bikfaya in the mountains to the east. Baptists in the capital city of Beirut were eager to win to Christ their friends and relatives in the villages from which they themselves had migrated to the metropolis.

In 1955 four cooperating churches formed the Lebanese Baptist Convention. With enlarged vision, the Convention formally joined the fellowship of the Baptist World Alliance in 1957. When in July of 1963 three thousand young people representing fifty-three countries converged on Beirut for the Sixth Baptist Youth World Conference, Baptists became known throughout the Arab world as a worldwide family of 25,000,000 freedom-loving, Bible-believing people.

The Land of Cedars

Blazoned on the red, white, and green flag of Lebanon, stamped on its coins, and used as a watermark on some of its paper money, the cedar tree serves admirably as the emblem of this modern nation. Down through the centuries the export of cedar wood has brought fame and wealth to the little country on the upper eastern shore of the Mediterranean. But Lebanon is renowned for more than its cedar trees.

You are able to read the words on this page because of an alphabet of letters whose origin can be traced back through ancient Lebanon (Phoenicia). Traders from Phoenicia carried a system of writing (evolved from Egyptian hieroglyphics) across the sea to Greece. From there, after further development, it was transported to Rome, to emerge after the passing of years as our modern alphabet.

Lebanon is unique among the turbulent countries of the Middle East in extending hands of friendship to the nations of the Western world while preserving close ties with Arab neighbors. It is unique also as the only Arab country in which a majority of the population is not Muslim but nominally Christian.

The Country

Only 4,015 square miles in area, Lebanon is one of the world's smallest countries, but important far out of proportion to its physical size. Bounded on the west by the Mediterranean Sea, on the north and east by Syria, on the south by Israel, its main port and capital (Beirut) is the gateway to the Holy Land. Thousands of modern pilgrims make Beirut a staging post by land, sea, and air on their way eastward and southward to points of biblical and archaeological interest. The city's modern hotels serve people from nations all over the world.

Through the centuries conquering armies have crossed and recrossed Lebanon, using international routes that have kept it linked to three continents—Africa, Asia, and Europe. Its name, Lebanon (from the same Semitic root as *liban*, meaning "milk"), means "white" and suggests its mountain ranges, from whose summits the snow never disappears. Only 135 miles long and about 35 miles wide, the country is dominated by two mountain ranges. The Lebanon range rises steeply less than a mile from the coast, with its highest peak, the Black Horn (10,000 feet) in the north, near the only substantial grove of cedar trees still left in this country famous for those trees in Old Testament days. The Anti-Lebanon range, which forms Lebanon's border with Syria, has as its highest peak Mount Hermon (9,300 feet), the traditional site of the transfiguration of Christ.

Between these mountain ranges lies the fertile Bekaa Valley, watered by two historically famous rivers whose sources near the archaeologically important city of Baalbek are only a few miles apart. One, the Liontes River, flows southward and enters the sea through an east-west fissure in the coastal mountain range near Tyre. The other, the Orontes River, flows northward through Syria and empties eventually into the Mediterranean near the biblical city of Antioch.

Called the Switzerland of the Middle East, Lebanon provides facilities for winter sports in season and an ideal vacation climate in summer. In late spring it is possible on the same day to ski on high mountain slopes and then, after only a half-hour's drive, to swim comfortably in the blue waters of the Mediterranean.

Cities

Famous among the biblical and ancient cities of Lebanon are Tyre, Sidon, Beirut, Byblos, Tripoli, and Baalbek.

Byblos, the modern town of Jubayl and the biblical city of Gebal, claims to be the oldest port in the world, but it is no longer used for commercial purposes. Famous in ancient times for its export of papyrus, which replaced clay tablets for writing, Byblos became the basis for the Greek word *biblion,* meaning "book." From this comes our English word "Bible."

Two whole chapters of Ezekiel's prophecy are devoted to the city of Tyre, called the "mother of cities." From its harbor sailed the Phoenician pioneers who established colonies on the shores of the Mediterranean Sea. Cadiz in Spain was established by Tyrian colonizers in 1100 B.C., and the Phoenicians sailed even farther onward into the Atlantic Ocean. The original city of Tyre was an island close to the mainland; today, the sea has receded, leaving a dry land crossing.

Sidon, according to tradition, was founded in 2750 B.C. by Sidon, the firstborn of Canaan, a grandson of Noah. Known for their skill as woodsmen, carpenters, and shipbuilders, the Sidonians of the ancient world were also famous for the quality and beauty of the glass they produced. The city is being commercially revived today because the Mediterranean terminus of the Trans-Arabian Pipe Line is nearby. The black gold of Saudi Arabia flows 1,070 miles across the desert to be transported to world markets by tankers loaded at Sidon.

Tripoli, so called because of its three distinct areas—the central town, harbor, and hillside section—is a comparatively young city, having been founded after 700 B.C. Flourishing today as the Mediterranean terminus of pipelines carrying oil from northern Iraq through the Syrian desert, its oil refinery provides most of the gasoline and other petroleum products consumed in Lebanon.

Baalbek (meaning "house" or "city" of Baal and called Heliopolis, city of the sun, by the Greeks), is famous for the ruins of the largest temple ever built to a heathen god. The Romans, who occupied Lebanon in 64 B.C., incorporated the local Phoenician god, Baal, into their religious system, calling him Jupiter. Using massive blocks of limestone from a nearby quarry, they erected huge temples to Jupiter, Diana, and Bacchus. To this day, engineers and archaeologists wonder how the immense blocks of stone, weighing as much as fourteen hundred tons, were raised into place.

One of the most beautiful port cities in the world, as well as one of the most cosmopolitan, is Beirut. Its harbor, continuously being expanded, is the busiest shipping center on the eastern Mediterranean seaboard, with the possible exception of Alexandria in Egypt. It is the largest port for goods entering or leaving Lebanon, Syria, and Jordan. Beirut's airport, opened in 1951 and designed for jet airliners before such aircraft were in commercial use, is typical of the progressive planning of Lebanese leaders. Once the home of a flourishing Roman law school established at the beginning of the third century after Christ, Beirut became the capital of the independent republic of Lebanon when the French mandate over the country ended in 1944.

Beirut is a city of contrasts with two quite distinct but equally exciting faces. Several factors have helped to make it the fourth largest financial center in the world:

FON H. SCOFIELD, JR.

Street scene, Beirut, Lebanon

Bedouin family, Taiybeh, Jordan

Dome of the Rock, Jerusalem

Registering patients, Baptist Hospital, Ajloun, Jordan

Musaitbi Baptist Church, Beirut, Lebanon

Baptist Book Store, Amman, Jordan

FON H. SCOFIELD, JR.

Dr. and Mrs. Merrill D. Moore, Jr.
Baptist Hospital, Gaza

Dr. Finlay M. Graham (left)
presenting diploma, Arab Baptist Theological Seminary

worldwide commercial establishments, local and foreign banks, insurance companies, a free zone at both harbor and airport (making possible the transit of goods for other destinations without payment of customs taxes), and an open money market for the free exchange of all currencies without government control. These, with the modern equipment, mechanical gadgets, radios, television sets, automatic telephone system, automobiles, jet planes, and multistoried office and apartment buildings owned and operated by Lebanese, suggest a Western orientation.

But take a stroll through the old marketplace and another face is evident. Porters carry huge loads on their backs. Youths carry on their heads boards laden with flat, pancake-shaped loaves of bread to be delivered from door to door to regular customers. Veiled women gracefully balance water jugs or baskets on their heads. Shoeshine boys run around looking for customers, their brass-covered boxes reflecting the bright sunlight. A middle-aged man in Western tailored suit with an Eastern fez as headgear, sips his Turkish coffee at a table in a sidewalk cafe. A housewife wearing a close-fitting skirt, sweater, high-heeled shoes, and nylon stockings seeks the best cut of meat at a bargain price as she argues volubly in Arabic with a mustached butcher who wears a long, red robe. East meets West daily in the city of Beirut, which tries to face both ways in order to keep in touch with a developing society while clinging to much of the tradition of the past. The age-old bargaining procedure of the Orient is still carried on even in shops that display the sign, "fixed prices."

Politically, too, Lebanon has endeavored to keep looking both ways, sometimes refusing to be involved in

East-West conflicts. Of necessity, however, she reveals her sympathy towards neighboring Arab countries, often serving as arbitrator in regional and international quarrels. This seemingly two-faced attitude in commerce and politics is no hypocritical stance. Lebanon's economic future still depends on her role as middleman for neighboring countries not yet in direct trade with the Western world. For economic reasons her doors must remain open to visiting tourists from the Americas, Africa, Europe, and Asia. When other Arab countries feel compelled to sever diplomatic ties with the West, Lebanon's interests dictate a policy of neutrality and arbitration, for the little country cannot afford to live in a state of isolation—diplomatic or economic, social or religious.

People

Despite continuous emigration to Canada, the United States, and South America, the resident population of Lebanon has increased in the last sixty years from a few hundred thousand to more than two million; and as many people of Lebanese origin live outside the country as in Lebanon itself. While the people belong basically to the Semitic race, Lebanese faces reflect traces of invasions and immigrations. They are descendants of a mixture of Phoenicians, Canaanites, Assyrians, Aramaeans, Babylonians, Egyptians, Hittites, Sumerians, Persians, Greeks, Romans, Turks, Mongols, Arabs, and eleventh-century Crusaders from Western Europe. In the narrow pass of the Dog River, near the Mediterranean coast a few miles north of Beirut, some twenty inscriptions in eight languages record the triumphs of conquerors who have marched through Lebanon since the fourteenth century before Christ came. Some of the warriors whose exploits have been inscribed there are Ramses II of Egypt, Esar-haddon of Nineveh, Nebuchadnezzar of Babylon, Emperior Marcus Aurelius of Rome, and Ottoman Sultan Salim—along with French, British, and Australian commanders of two world wars.

The clearest population differences in Lebanon are those of religion. Religious freedom is guaranteed all citizens by the constitution. There is no state religion. The nation is made up of a unique complex of religious persuasions. Just over half the population is nominally Christian—Maronite Catholics, Greek Orthodox, Armenian Orthodox, Syrian Orthodox, Uniate[2] and Latin Catholics,[3] and some Evangelicals. The balance of the population is Muslim and Druse, with a dwindling number of Jews. About a dozen synagogues in Beirut bear out the fact of religious freedom as a fundamental principle of the Lebanese constitution.

Religion plays a more vital part in the political, social, and cultural life of Lebanese people than in their private lives. The country is divided into five governorates (counties), most of them comprising mixed religious populations; but within these governorates, many towns and villages are inhabited by one predominating religious group. A Muslim village is identified by its minaret from which the muezzin's[4] stirring call to prayer awakens the inhabitants daily before sunrise. Maronite communities are evident from their wayside shrines containing statues of the Virgin or saints and from the number of well-fed, black-bonneted, and robed priests making their way to substantial stone churches. Druse communities are identified by their white-turbaned, black-bearded religious leaders. Other religious divisions are not so easily identified, but are in themselves closely knit, traditional communities. Evangelicals, few in numbers but influential, play an important role in the country's educational, cultural, and professional life. Even Jews have their own community in Beirut.

Religious barriers tend to break down in the cities. Partnerships in business ventures involving Christians, Muslims, and sometimes Jews, are not uncommon.

Baptist Converts from Various Religious Backgrounds

The Muslim faith in Lebanon is represented by its two main sects, Sunni (Orthodox) and Shiite (or followers of Ali). Usually allied with these politically is the breakaway Druse sect. The prime minister of Lebanon is appointed by the president from the ranks of the Sunnis, the nation's largest Muslim group, who regard themselves as orthodox. Shiite Muslims in Lebanon are slightly less numerous than Sunnis, but wield considerable political influence. From among them the chamber of deputies elects the speaker of the parliament. The Druses, of uncertain origin, have drifted far from the beliefs of their Muslim forebears. Tinged with animism, their beliefs include the doctrine of the transmigration of souls. Hardy, energetic, and warlike, they are fiercely independent and extremely loyal to their own people. Perhaps no group in the whole Arab world is more difficult to win to Christ, but God is at work in their midst. Ayoub Naim is an example.

Born into a Druse family, Ayoub was stricken at an early age by a disease that left his eyesight impaired. Gradually he became completely blind. Hearing of a school for blind boys where he could learn to read, he became a boarding student. Soon his intelligent mind and nimble fingers grasped the Braille alphabet and he became one of the best students in the school, which was administered by kindly British missionaries. The main textbook of the school was the Bible. Ayoub memorized Scripture passages, and as he hid God's Word in his heart he became conscious of his need of an inner light. One day a missionary explained to him the significance of Jesus, the Light of the world, and Ayoub's heart was responsive. God's plan of salvation became clearer and clearer to him until he accepted Christ as his Saviour.

Skilled in the art of making and repairing wickerwork chairs, Ayoub set up his own business when he was graduated from the blind school. He soon became known for his honesty, the high quality of his work, and his zeal and joy in witnessing for Christ. He has led several young men to Christ and has encouraged others to enter the gospel ministry.

Looking for a spiritual home where he might unite in fellowship with other believing Christians, Ayoub was introduced to Baptists. Satisfied that their way of life was scriptural, he was baptized and has been a faithful member of the Musaitbi Baptist Church in Beirut for more than thirty years. About fifteen years ago his church decided to ordain deacons, and Ayoub was one of those elected. Possessed of an amazing memory, he delights to expound the Word of God from the pulpit, in Sunday School classrooms, and in home Bible-study groups. He often exclaims, "Thank God for my blindness through which I was introduced to Jesus, the Light of the world."

Undoubtedly the most influential single religious group in Lebanon is the Maronite Church, one of the Christian sects. Monks from this sect fled for refuge from

Syria to Lebanon in the fifth century to escape persecution because their beliefs concerning the person of
Christ differed somewhat from those of Catholicism.
Seeking relief from Muslim persecution, Maronite Christians in the twelfth century gained the protection of
the Pope by accepting Roman Catholic leadership, but
they clung to their own beliefs until the eighteenth century. The Arabic language continued to be used for
their church services, with Mass being read in the
ancient Syriac. The parish priest still retained the right
to take a wife before ordination, a practice on which
the entire parish insists. This warlike group of mountain people was never subjugated by Muslim rulers.

Since the independence of Lebanon as a republic in
1944 its president has always been elected from the
Maronite Christian part of the population in secret ballot
by two-thirds majority of the Chamber of Deputies. The
president appoints the prime minister and other cabinet
ministers on a basis that insures a proper representation
of all religious faiths.

Prominent among Lebanese Baptists is Saleem Sharouk, now retired from active service as a pastor, but
still witnessing faithfully to all who visit in his home.
Born of Maronite parents in a village near Sidon in
south Lebanon, Saleem as a boy assisted the village priest
on Sundays and during feast days. So dedicated was
he that the people of his village voted to nominate him
for training in the priesthood. For economic reasons
he moved to the city of Beirut and became a shoemaker
by trade.

A handsome youth, ruddy complexioned with reddish
hair and a bristling mustache, Saleem won the heart of
Mona, a young Maronite maiden from a mountain village

on the Beirut-Damascus highway. Her father agreed to the marriage and an official engagement took place. After some months, during which Saleem was preparing a home for his future bride, a richer suitor, Mona's own cousin, asked for her, and her father wanted to break off the engagement with Saleem.

In the meantime, Mona had been attending a Lutheran boarding school run by German deaconesses in Beirut. Occasionally she would send a letter to Saleem by a blind man who repaired wicker chairs. This man was a Baptist with a reputation of being a walking concordance of the Bible. As he delivered letters to Mona's fiance he seized every opportunity to give him a tract and speak to him of Christ. Saleem objected to his persistence but felt obliged to give him a hearing as long as he was willing to deliver letters to Mona and bring back her replies.

The blind man brought him a copy of the New Testament in Arabic, and Saleem promised to read it. He came in his reading to the tenth chapter of Hebrews, verse thirty-one, "It is a fearful thing to fall into the hands of the living God," and his Maronite self-righteousness received a rude shock.

When her father persisted in his intention to marry her off to her rich cousin, Mona agreed to elope with Saleem—an almost unheard-of-thing in Lebanon in those days. Through the help of a sympathetic friend, they were secretly married by a Maronite priest, who wondered why those two young people refused to participate in the customary rite of confession before the ceremony.

Saleem took his bride home and that very night told her that he could not deceive her any longer. "You may think that you have married a Maronite Catholic," he said, "but you are wrong." He took his New Testament and explained to her how Christ had changed his life. Joyfully, Mona shared with him her own experience of Christ in the Lutheran school.

"But that is not all," said Saleem, and he told her he had become convinced that believer's baptism by immersion was the only true scriptural baptism. As they continued to study the New Testament together, Mona also became convinced. Together they visited Pastor Said Jureidini and later were baptized into the fellowship of the Beirut Baptist Church. As they dedicated themselves to God, Saleem's prayer was, "Lord, twenty-three years I have spent in the service of the devil, but from now on I serve only you." More than fifty years of fruitful service testify that Saleem has faithfully fulfilled his baptismal vow.

When the shoemaking trade experienced a slump, Saleem became a taxi driver. Wherever he went he gave his Christian testimony. On Sundays he used his taxi only to drive people, without charge, to the Baptist church in order that they might hear the gospel and accept his Saviour as their own. When Baptist missionaries went to live in Beirut in 1948, more than half the Baptist church members were converts of this dedicated witness. These were handpicked fruit, firmly grounded in the Word, proud to be Baptists.

The Greek Orthodox Church, the largest single Christian denomination in the Arab world, ranks second in Lebanon. Traditionally, the deputy prime minister is elected from this group. Numbering 150,000, Lebanese Greek Orthodox Christians claim an unbroken tie with Christianity of the first century after Christ. But the Greek Orthodox Church in Lebanon today is a "sleeping" church. Most of the members of Baptist churches in the Arab world, especially in Lebanon and Jordan, are from a Greek Orthodox background. Elias Saleebi an eloquent Baptist preacher, is a grandnephew of the Greek Orthodox archbishop of Beirut.

The village of Aindara, near the top of the pass that cuts through the Lebanon range of mountains and provides the main road link between Beirut and Damascus, is known for its apple orchards and its hardy mountain villagers. Perhaps because their village is located in a predominantly Druse part of the country, the people have clung tenaciously to their Orthodox views. Consequently, they resist all attempts to reach them with the evangelical gospel's demand of personal commitment to Christ. The largest single family group of this picturesque village is the Haddad family.

After completing elementary school in Aindara, Dahir Haddad was sent as a boarder to the Friends (Quaker) High School in another town. At this renowned institution, Scripture lessons were the order of the day. Although the young boy was not personally introduced to Christ, the seed of God's Word was planted in his heart. When he returned to his native village as a schoolteacher, took himself a wife, and established a home, he gave the Bible a prominent place in his family. God blessed him with five sons and one daughter.

The third and fourth sons in this family were employed with the company responsible for installation and maintenance of the transdesert oil pipeline that terminates near the Lebanese port of Sidon. The fourth son, Abdul Messih, became an electrician at the Sidon plant and there found Christ through the witness of a Palestinian refugee who, before 1948, had run an evangelical printing plant in Jerusalem. Boulos, the third son, worked as an accountant in the Beirut office of the pipeline company.

Rather reluctantly, Boulos agreed to go with Abdul Messih to a revival meeting in the Musaitbi Baptist Church, Beirut. Impressed and convicted by what he heard in the first service, Boulos continued to attend until he responded one night to the gospel invitation. He and Abdul Messih were later baptized into the fellowship of the church. They have had the joy of seeing their mother, two other brothers, their only sister, their paternal uncle, and several cousins take their places in the ranks of Baptist witnesses in Lebanon. Their father also confessed Christ as his Saviour before his death a few years ago. Though still employed with the pipeline company, Boulos serves as pastor of a Baptist church in a suburb of Beirut. His church established a mission congregation in Aindara, which in 1967 was organized into an independent Baptist church.

The youngest brother in the family, a brilliant young man named Wadia, is a professor at the American University of Beirut. In December, 1967, he was elected president of the Lebanon Baptist Convention, the first layman to serve in that office. As a member of the University Baptist Church, the burden of his heart is to reach for Christ the international student body of the strategically placed institution where he teaches. Through discussion groups, Bible studies, weekend conferences, personal contacts on the campus, and in the classroom, Dr. Wadia Haddad is seeking to bring young men and women (from some fifty countries) of the colleges of Beirut to a face-to-face encounter with the living Christ. In this ministry he continues the pioneering witness of veteran missionary Lillie Hundley, who, after long service in China and Hawaii, devoted her last term to student work in Beirut.

Missionary Bill Trimble, first pastor of the University Baptist Church (English-speaking), had the privilege of baptizing a Pakistani graduate student of Muslim background who was brought to Christ through the ministry of Miss Hundley. Dr. Haddad continues to work in close cooperation with this church, where James and Elizabeth Kirkendall now serve a cosmopolitan community of diverse religious backgrounds. Won to Christ while studying in Beirut, student graduates from many countries return to their homelands to share their experience with fellow countrymen.

The Greek Catholic Church of Lebanon, numbering 100,000 members, acknowledges the sovereignty of the Roman Catholic Pope but retains the Church's Eastern rites and uses the Arabic language in most of its procedures. Six of the ninety-nine members of the Lebanese parliament's chamber of deputies are traditionally Greek Catholics.

Rizcallah Constantine was appropriately named by his Greek Catholic parents. His given name means "boon" or "blessing." Gifted with a good singing voice, he was popular with his schoolmates and was a leader of the gang from his early teen years. The conversion of his aunt's husband, an ardent Communist, changed the direction of Rizcallah's life. The transformation of his uncle was so evident that the whole community of Greek Catholics in the area of Beirut where he lived was startled. It caused Rizcallah to begin to attend Baptist services, and during a revival meeting he made a profession of faith in Christ. Immediately dedicating his talents to the Lord's service, he began to take an interest in teaching in Sunday School and leading the singing in the Musaitbi Baptist Church.

Making his living in a dry-cleaning business and as a signwriter, Rizcallah did not have much free time, but what time he had he put to good use in intensive Bible study. When a door opened for mission work in Bikfaya, a mountain summer resort, the church asked him and his wife to enter the new field of service. The work was hard. Unable to make a dent among the adult population, the young couple concentrated their efforts on children and young people.

Sunday School work always had appealed to Rizcallah. The young people and children responded to his ministry. Bikfaya Baptist Church stands today as a monument to their persistent and fruitful witnessing where others tried and failed. The majority of the members of this church have been won through Sunday School. Two young men have been called to the gospel ministry. One was a member of the first graduating class from the Arab Baptist Theological Seminary before his pastor (who has since graduated also) had an opportunity to attend. The Bikfaya Baptist Church has established three congregations in surrounding villages.

Hearts hungry for the Word of God have been reached and won for Christ. They constitute the nucleus of local churches in an ever-widening ministry. These converts from different religious groups are helping to answer the insistent plea, "How shall they hear?"

Notes

[1] "Jureidini" is a well-known Greek Orthodox family name in a village near Beirut. *Said* means "happy." See *Photographer in*

Lebanon: The Story of Said Jureidini by McRae recently published by Broadman Press.

[2] Named for their union with Rome, though they still cling to their own liturgy and rites and elect their own prelates.

[3] Using the Latin language for their services.

[4] The muezzin, meaning "announcer" or "broadcaster," is chosen for the quality of his voice. Resonant voices are most in demand for the office, though tape recordings have made the task quite impersonal.

4
Hearing Through
Deeds Of Mercy

The modern Baptist witness in Lebanon has been promoted largely through direct, personal evangelism—a
spontaneous overflow from those who have experienced
the saving power of the gospel in their own lives to
those who have felt its need. Unique in the Arab world
in the freedom of religion afforded all of its citizens,
Lebanon lends itself to the purely evangelistic communi-
cation of the gospel. Perhaps the very diversity of religious persuasions among its people makes a fruitful
evangelistic testimony possible.

But direct personal evangelism is not possible in every
part of the Arab world. Where Islam reigns supreme
and traditional barriers to the Christian faith have been
strengthened by centuries of prejudice and misinterpre-
tation, genuine Christian love must be expressed in
decidely. practical ways. Where the church is forbidden
to communicate directly through preaching, other meth-
ods must be used. In some areas an educational type
of ministry has been necessary to open doors, in others
a medical ministry.

Today Southern Baptist missionaries express the compassion of Christ in a ministry of healing in three different areas of the Arab world: the Hashemite Kingdom
of Jordan; the country of Yemen, claimed by both royalist

and republican forces, neither really democratic; and the much disputed Gaza Strip, whose refugee camps are a hotbed of political and economic unrest. In these countries the healing ministry of Baptist hospitals, staffed by national as well as missionary personnel, declares that God is love and says it more eloquently than the preached word, which is so often misinterpreted. It declares that God is concerned with the physical and mental as well as the spiritual needs of suffering humanity.

It was not until after World War II that Southern Baptists began seriously to consider work in the Arab world. Missionaries sent out in the 1940's studied the Arabic language and explored opportunities for service. Some of them hoped to establish medical work in the Arabian peninsula. However, the door of entrance into Arabia proper remained tightly closed, and God led them elsewhere.

A British doctor and a small group of believers had established an evangelical hospital in the Gilead of the Old Testament, identified today as the Ajloun area of the Hashemite Kingdom of Jordan. They served faithfully for several years, but financial straits threatened to close the hospital, and Southern Baptists were asked to accept responsibility for the work. Thus it happened that Baptist missionaries entered Jordan instead of the Arabian peninsula, beginning their work with the Ajloun hospital in 1952.

The Hashemite Kingdom of Jordan

Jordan has a history dating back to ancient times. Ruled by a succession of people from early Canaanite days to the long Ottoman Turkish domination which ended with World War I, the nation of today reflects the culture of great civilizations which have left their mark on country, people, and monuments.

History and Geography

Although the Hashemite Kingdom of Jordan has existed in its own right since 1920, it was in 1949 that it assumed its present name. After World War I, Transjordan, a Syrian district of the former Ottoman Empire, was placed with Palestine under a British mandate. Abdullah, son of the king who ruled Arabia's northwestern province, was appointed ruler. As Transjordan, the country was granted full independence in 1946. At that time the whole realm lay east of the Jordan River. In 1950, Arab Palestine, the area that was not occupied then by Israel west of the river, was formally annexed by Abdullah. In this way he gained territory on both sides of the river. The territory on the west bank was taken by Israel in the brief war of June, 1967.

Bounded on the north by Syria, on the northeast by Iraq, on the east and south by Saudi Arabia, and on the west by Israel, Jordan is almost completely landlocked. Its coastline consists of a few miles on the Red Sea around its one port of Aqaba, between Israel and the Arabian border.

Two important elements have helped determine Jordan's history. The first of these is security. Down through the centuries the land area has acted as a buffer between the desert and a progressive civilization. Archaeological mounds testify to the security given in ancient times by fortified cities. During five centuries under Rome a network of roads and frontier strongholds kept bedouin marauders at bay. The famous Arab

Legion, now officially known as the Arab Army, has continued in modern times to play an important role in Jordan.

Trade has been a second determinative factor. Jordan's political and economic history has been closely linked with caravans from southern Arabia, bearing spices northward to Damascus and eastward to Baghdad. The King's Highway of Numbers 20:17, replaced in the second century by a Roman road, followed the same route as the modern paved road from Aqaba through Amman to Damascus and other points north. Commerce came this way from India to Rome. After the caravan trade declined from the fifteenth century on, and produce from the Orient was diverted by way of the Red Sea through Alexandria, this old trade route continued to be used in a different role. Muslim pilgrim traffic through Jordan to Mecca flourished when a railroad was laid by the Ottoman Turks to link Damascus with Medina.

Cities

The history of a country is revealed in the history of its cities. Some of the most ancient cities of the world are located in Jordan.

The history of Amman, Jordan's capital, dates back to Old Testament days and earlier. Situated east of the Jordan River and forty-five miles northeast of Jerusalem, it was the ancient capital of the biblical kingdom of Ammon (Rabbah Ammon in 1 Chron. 20:1). In the third century before Christ its name was changed to Philadelphia. As part of the Decapolis (the ten cities —Roman colonies—of Transjordan, mentioned in Matt. 4:25) it flourished under Roman rule. For political reasons, King Abdullah made it his capital in modern times. From a small bedouin camp fifty years ago, it has grown to a busy metropolis of almost three hundred and fifty thousand inhabitants, with power plants, printing shops, a royal palace, government buildings, several schools, and in one of its suburbs a university.

Jerash, in the beautiful Gilead mountains twenty miles from Amman, claims attention as the best preserved of all Roman colonies of the Middle East. Also part of the Decapolis, it flourished during the first three centuries after Christ.

Petra, in the south of Jordan, provides one of the world's great travel experiences. This rose-tinted city of the Nabataeans was lost in its craggy, protective mountain environment for five hundred years. Rainbow-tinted sandstone rocks, and buildings carved from the mountainside, make it one of the most photogenic attractions offered to tourists anywhere.

Other modern towns and cities of Jordan contend for consideration. Zerka, fifteen miles northeast of Amman, is rapidly developing into the nation's main industrial center and the site of the Arab Army's largest camp. Irbid, near the Syrian border, is a market town in the most fertile wheat-growing area of the eastern Jordanian highlands. Roads branch out from Irbid to Amman in the south, Damascus in the north, and the Jordan Valley in the west.

People and Economics

The population of Jordan is made up of people with dissimilar backgrounds, each group preserving its distinctive origin. Arab descendants of bedouin tribes are in the majority, but there are minority groups of Circassian,

Turkish, Druse, and Armenian people. Nomadic and seminomadic bedouin continue to live in tents and to maintain their tribal customs.

As a result of Arab-Israeli conflict since 1947, an influx of Arab refugees has increased the population of the country. Astute students of Middle East affairs wonder whether Jordan has absorbed these refugees from the area formerly called Palestine, or is being absorbed by them. They have been a mixed blessing. The majority of them are still in refugee camps and their intense Palestinian nationalism is continuously being exploited by political leaders throughout the Arab world. This nationalism is expressed in an emotion that arises partly from wounded pride and revengeful feelings, and partly out of personal suffering and loss. Among the blessings is their active desire for progress along western lines, which has provided the spur for social and educational advances. The refugees have proved to be the leaven of restless enterprise in the sturdy but somewhat complacent Jordanian community.

Heavily subsidized since its foundation, the Hashemite Kingdom of Jordan lacks an abundance of raw materials and sources of energy basic to industrial development. Some strides have been made, however, in soap and cooking-oil manufacturing, in the cement industry, in tobacco and food processing, and in the mining and production of phosphates. High-grade marble quarries await some enterprising citizen's exploitation on a larger scale.

Religion

About 90 percent of Jordanians are Muslim, most of them of the Sunni sect. The nominally Christian minority

—consisting of Greek Orthodox, Greek Catholic, Roman or Latin Catholic, and evangelical communities—are scattered throughout the country but predominate in the cities of Salt, Madaba, and Kerak. Traditionally oriented and tightly integrated, these religious communities raise automatic barriers to the innovations of a Baptist witness which cuts across all man-made traditions. The Baptist faith gives an opportunity to all, of whatever historic community, to accept the lordship of Christ and be integrated into a democratic religious society.

Jordan's people, like those in other Arab countries, but more so, are facing the problem of transition from the nomadic to the urban way of life, from traditional to modern values. Dependence on the solidarity of the family group is being questioned. An attitude of personal independence and the need of individual adjustment to a changing situation predominates. Still, some prized virtues—hospitality, dignity, honor, and pride—remain in Jordanian society.

Baptists in Jordan

Into this complex of political, social, economic, and religious elements, Southern Baptists have penetrated with the witness of the gospel. They aim not to win the Jordanians away from any national, political, or cultural ideology, but to win their allegiance to Christ, the Lord of life.

Balm in Gilead

The Ajloun hospital located in Gilead, the mount of the prophet Elijah, became the responsibility of Southern Baptists in 1952. Outpatient clinics, a school of nursing, and two primary schools operated by the former administration of the hospital, were avenues through which Southern Baptists began their ministry of healing, teaching, and preaching in this northern area of Jordan.

Ajloun Baptist Hospital is not in a metropolitan city, nor even in a village, but out in the country. Even so, there is no part of the Hashemite Kingdom of Jordan untouched by its witness. Patients have come to the hospital from 250 cities, towns, and villages. No one enters and leaves the hospital without receiving a copy of the New Testament in Arabic and without hearing the plan of salvation explained by members of the hospital staff. The effective outreach of the Baptist medical ministry in Jordan as a medium for the spread of the gospel was clearly demonstrated in the first simultaneous evangelistic campaign promoted by Jordanian Baptists in the spring of 1967. People were reached in villages where seeds of the gospel had been sown by the medical ministry of the Ajloun hospital, where missionary doctors John and Ruth Roper and others engaged in the medical ministry of the Ajloun hospital.

A Modern Simon the Sorcerer

Many of the inhabitants of Kifringi, a local government center some ten miles from Ajloun, have been patients in the Baptist Hospital. Abu Ibrahim (meaning "father of Abraham"; Arab parents are usually designated as father or mother of their oldest son), one of the best-known citizens of the village, was a hardened character whose daughter Wardi served years ago as a graduate nurse at the Ajloun hospital and while there came to know Christ as her Saviour. How her father's wickedness grieved her! Not content with a life of debauchery, he began to delve into sorcery, claiming ability to predict future events, and writing verses from the Koran or the New Testament (for Muslim or Christian customers, respectively) as charms to help sterile women bear children to their divorce-threatening husbands or, even more tragic, to be used to bring misfortune to enemies. With all this, Abu Ibrahim was arrogantly self-righteous.

A son-in-law of Abu Ibrahim was taken to the Ajloun hospital with little hope of recovery from a complication of diabetes and heart disease. He was an avowed atheist and repeated his conviction that there is no God. "If there is a God, why am I suffering like this?" he asked. His wife, a believing Christian, prayed for him and had the inner assurance that her husband would repent before his death. Kind treatment in the hospital softened his hard attitude and, at first for want of something else to do, he began to read the New Testament. God's Spirit gradually applied the Word to his heart and he saw himself as a sinner. In penitence he cried to God for mercy and his prayer was heard. Soon he began to witness to all who visited him, testifying of the love of God, whose existence he had so long denied.

Abu Ibrahim was among those who visited his son-in-law in the hospital. Although he was impressed with the change he saw in his relative, he continued on in his own wicked way. When special evangelistic services were held in Kifringi as part of the simultaneous campaign of 1967, one of his companions was converted. In the movement of the Spirit that swept through the village, many notable sinners found peace with God.

They began to pray for Abu Ibrahim who, with his usual show of bravado, agreed to attend the services, assuring his friends that whatever the preacher might say would have no effect on him. During the first sermon, he heard the evangelist describe those without Christ as condemned sinners.

"I'm not a sinner," Abu Ibrahim shouted from his seat, "and do not dare call me one."

At the close of that service the preacher and the congregation covenanted together not to cease praying for Abu Ibrahim until he should come to his senses and to Christ. On the third night of his attendance at the revival meeting he felt the stinging, convicting power of the Holy Spirit.

"Is there any hope for a sinner like me?" he asked in anguish. "If there is, please pray for me."

After the close of the service the evangelist pointed out to him verses of Scripture that assure sinful men of God's reception of everyone truly repentant. Abu Ibrahim had always been too proud to make any public display of emotion, but tears began to flow down his rough cheeks as he realized the power of God's love for him. Immediately he began to speak with others of what God had done for him, visiting different Baptist churches to give his personal testimony.

A few days afterwards a Muslim woman customer came to seek his help. "My husband is theatening to divorce me because I have borne no children," she declared. "Please write me a verse that will cure me." She handed him the equivalent of fifteen dollars to pay for his service.

"I have stopped that evil practice," Abu Ibrahim answered, "but I know something more effective—prayer.

Pray to God, and I will pray for you also. He is able to meet your need."

The message of God's healing power, physical and spiritual, goes out in ever-widening circles from the Ajloun Baptist Hospital. Hundreds of villages have been reached with the "balm in Gilead to heal the sin-sick soul." There are hundreds more where the gospel has not yet been preached. How shall they hear?

Stormy Days

All is not plain sailing for Baptist missionaries in Jordan. Their lives have been in danger when mobs ruthlessly and wantonly have caused damage throughout the country. A wave of antiwesternism followed the Suez Canal crisis of 1956. In January of 1957 gangs of hooligans comprised of high-school students, incited by pro-Communist and pro-Nasser teachers, attacked the hospital in Ajloun. The male nurses' dormitory outside the compound was set on fire and the outpatients' clinic just inside the main entrance was entered and damaged. Fortunately, no lives were lost.

The attackers left as suddenly as they had appeared, apparently rather ashamed of themselves for having tried to destroy the only institution providing aid for the sick and injured in an area of more than a hundred villages. During the attack, Dr. August Lovegren, 'the only missionary doctor on hand, calmly continued to aid a woman in the throes of childbirth, while his wife, Alta Lee, witnessed to a group of women in the hospital compound. Public reaction was strongly in favor of the missionaries. Leaders of the attack were sought out, but the hospital administration refused to press charges against them. Damaged buildings were repaired and the hospital staff determined to manifest the mind of Christ toward their persecutors. Since that time some of the attackers have come to the hospital for treatment and have indicated their sincere regret for their earlier destructive action.

The Gaza Strip

In 1954 the Church Missionary Society (Anglican) asked Southern Baptists to consider taking over its hospital in the city of Gaza. The British missionaries were unable to continue operating the institution, which they had founded three quarters of a century before to meet the needs of patients from all over the south of Palestine.

The Gaza Strip, forty miles south of Tel Aviv, is on the Mediterranean coast of what was known until 1948 as Palestine. The narrow coastal strip, twenty-five miles long by five miles wide, is occupied by about 350,000 people, the majority of them Arab refugees forced out of their homeland by war.

The city of Gaza is mentioned in both the Old and New Testaments. Biblical maps show it in the heart of Philistine country where David found refuge when fleeing from Saul. Here Samson, after his eyes had been put out by his enemies, pulled down the temple of Dagon, in the act destroying his tormentors and himself. Not far from the city is Khan Yunis (Jonah's Inn) where, according to Muslim tradition, Jonah was cast up by the whale.

During their occupation of Palestine the Romans used Gaza as their port for the southern part of the country. Sections of marble columns in the Baptist hospital compound testify to the rule of Rome from the first century before Christ. One such column was used for a time as a pulpit stand in the hospital chapel.

A Miracle of Healing

Today, the Gaza Baptist Hospital, its school of nursing, and one Baptist church organized in 1960, constitute the only evangelical Christian witness to the people of the Gaza Strip. Miracles of healing have taken place within its walls. Lou Ellyn Coffey, a missionary journeyman who served for two years as a nurse in Gaza Baptist Hospital, relates a thrilling eyewitness experience:

"I was in the nursing classroom in our Baptist hospital in Gaza when one of the students came running to the door, calling, 'Come quickly, Miss Coffey. Dr. Dorr needs you in the emergency room.'

"I ran to the emergency room and on my way wondered what kind of case would await me there. I knew it must be very serious if Dr. David Dorr, our hospital director, had been to see the case. I thought possibly it would be a bleeding woman or a burned child, since we see many such cases. But when I arrived I was not prepared for what I saw. On the floor lay a young bedouin lad about twelve years old. He was bleeding profusely, and examination showed he had no blood pressure or pulse. He had been run over by a train, and his right arm and leg were barely attached by a little skin that remained intact.

" 'I don't know if we can save him or not,' Dr. Dorr said. 'He's very sick and we will have to amputate both the arm and the leg.'

"It all seemed so hopeless to me that I looked at Dr. Dorr and said, 'Why don't we just leave him? He's about to die. Who will want him deformed? What's one more life anyway?' I know now that was the wrong

way to think or feel but, honestly, that was exactly
how I felt at the time. I knew he would have a difficult life if he lived.

"Dr. Dorr looked steadily at me and said, 'We are
here to try to save lives, no matter how hopeless it may
seem to us. We cannot judge life or death. We must do
all we can to save this boy.' I knew deep down in my
heart that he was right.

"We quickly made preparation for surgery. Dr. Dorr
and our other missionary physician, Dr. Merrill Moore,
scrubbed the case. Several times during the operation it
seemed that the young boy would not live; but, amazingly, he did. Then, for the next few days, as we kept
constant vigil over him, he steadily improved.

"All of us knew it was a real miracle that he lived.
An even greater miracle was that he began to walk
with one crutch. This was amazing because he had
the right arm and right leg amputated. It was most
difficult for him to learn to balance himself.

"Even though he improved, and all of our hospital
staff was overjoyed and happy, I kept wondering why
God had spared him. Then one day I knew. I went
to his bedside and he was reading a Gospel of John
in Arabic. He was very much interested in it. We
began to talk and as we did I was able to share with
him the good news of Jesus Christ. He had never
heard the gospel before and was most receptive to it.
He did not at that moment accept Jesus as his Saviour,
but he has continued to read the Bible. I feel that one
reason his life was spared so amazingly was so he could
hear the good news he'd never heard before. I believe
that someday he will be a real follower of Jesus Christ,
and his testimony will be used to lead many others to

Christ."

Two days before this bedouin boy was discharged from the hospital he accepted Christ as his Saviour. He has been back several times for a checkup, smiling from ear to ear and assuring our missionaries that Christ lives in his heart. Saved physically and spiritually, he is a living testimony to the Baptist witness in Gaza.

Staying with It

Gaza, periodically in the news because of border clashes between Israeli and Egyptian armed forces, could be a frustrating post for anyone not definitely called to missionary service. The Strip has changed hands three times in the past twelve years. The Baptist hospital, to the everlasting credit of our missionaries, has stayed open regardless of which government was in control.

When fresh hostilities broke out between Israel and the Arab countries on June 5, 1967, the Baptist Hospital in Gaza was in the thick of things. As a precautionary measure, all missionaries and dependents except the two male doctors had been evacuated. Realizing that their presence was vitally important to the welfare of the people in the area, Dr. Dorr and Dr. Moore felt that it was their duty to stay on and keep the hospital functioning. The national staff watched Dr. Dorr's every movement, fearing he would be leaving; for if this happened, the hospital would cease to function. It was felt that if the doctors left in the time of emergency, irreparable harm would be done to the reputation of the hospital, and the possibility of reestablishing it later would be remote.

From May 28, when other missionary personnel and

children were evacuated, until the outbreak of hostilities on June 5, Dr. Dorr put his hospital in a state of readiness to receive and treat large numbers of casualties. Extra beds, mattresses, medical supplies, and food were accumulated. For two days, June 5 and 6, the hospital was the center of intensive mortar and shell fire from Israeli forces who were trying to knock out Egyptian guns in the vicinity. Four shells landed and exploded in the hospital compound, injuring one staff member but causing little damage to buildings. The hospital continued to function, full to overflowing.

The main government hospital in Gaza was placed under heavy security after the Israeli Army captured the city of Gaza. A number of United Arab Republic and Palestinian Liberation Army officers had tried to evade capture by masquerading as members of the hospital staff or as patients. As a result, patients normally admitted to the Government hospital were sent to the Baptist hospital. The burden on Dr. Dorr and Dr. Moore and their staff was increased enormously. Water was scarce and a general current failure necessitated the use of a secondary lighting system, but emergency operations were successfully performed during the height of the bombardment. A United Nations official who was present in Gaza during the conflict declared that these men were worthy of the highest public recognition and of receiving a medal for their bravery and devotion to duty. Their reward is the satisfaction of having showed the love of Christ to people when they needed it most.

Why do Southern Baptist missionaries continue to live in the restricted area of the Gaza Strip, constantly under the pressure of conflicting political emotions that are ready to flare up without warning, suffering the pain of separation from their children (at the age of eleven or twelve sent to Beirut or Alexandria or further afield for their secondary education), often discouraged because of the comparatively few who respond to the claims of Christ? The answer is simple: Thousands of people there need Christ. They will not hear unless Christian missionaries, impelled by divine compassion, come there to tell them.

The effect of Baptist witness in Gaza is much wider than the small number of baptized church members would indicate. Nursing students, both male and female, won to Christ during their years of training in the Gaza Baptist School of Nursing, have graduated, some to continue on the permanent staff, but most to go further afield—to Kuwait and other Persian Gulf states, to Saudi Arabia, and to Yemen—where only a flickering candle of gospel light shines in the spiritual darkness.

The winning of Muslims in the Middle East, the hard core of Islamic territory, involves difficulties that are, humanly speaking, insurmountable. Muslims are not easily won to Christ; yet, they are being won—not in large groups, but one by one. On the wall of the outpatient waiting room of the Gaza Baptist Hospital are inscribed the words of one who gave his life that Muslims might have eternal life: "Come unto me, all ye that labour and are heavy laden, and I will give you rest" (Matt. 11:28). At the main door of the Ajloun Baptist Hospital, engraved in stone, is the ultimate expression of sacrificial love: "For God so loved the world, that he gave his only begotten Son, that whosoever believeth in him should not perish, but have everlasting life" (John 3:16). Only as the compassion of Christ is truly demonstrated in the lives of his followers will the people of the Arab world accept him as Saviour.

How shall they hear? Sometimes hearing properly comes only through seeing clearly.

Yemen

Who would be foolish enough or daring enough to leave the comparative security of a well-established medical institution, in a situation in which he enjoyed prestige and respect as a leading member of the community, and take his family to a country that traditionally bans Christians of all nationalities and sects? Yemen is nearly 100 percent Muslim. When a Swedish traveler died there in an accident a few years ago, such an outcry arose at the thought of his "infidel" body being buried in holy Yemeni Muslim soil that he had to be interred secretly at night in open country in an unmarked grave.

The pioneering spirit is by no means dead among Southern Baptist missionaries. Dr. James Young, Jr., while director of the Baptist Hospital in Gaza, became interested in Yemen. He began to investigate the possibility of medical mission work in that country, where for thirteen centuries there has been practically no Christian witness. After persistent inquiry and patient waiting, he obtained a visa for an exploratory visit. He discovered that Yemen, medically speaking, is one of the neediest lands in the world. In the entire country there is not one Yemeni doctor practicing medicine.

There seemed to be no hope, from a human standpoint, of gaining permission for any type of Christian mission work in Yemen. But Dr. Young refused to take no as an answer. His friendly approach won the support of the Minister of Health. After much negotiation, a miracle took place in the form of an official invitation to the

Foreign Mission Board of the Southern Baptist Convention to undertake a medical ministry in what is officially known today as the Arab Republic of Yemen.

The Country

Yemen was a little-known area until very recent years. It gave practically no encouragement to travelers, and being fairly self-supporting it required little contact with the outside world.

Covering an area of seventy-five thousand square miles, Yemen lies in the southwest corner of the Arabian Peninsula. It is bordered on the north and east by Saudi Arabia, on the south by the Federation of South Arabia, and on the west by the Red Sea. Arabs of North and South Arabian origin comprise the bulk of its population of about five million. However, the hot coastal plain is occupied by a mixed group of people of African origin, with Somalis and Ethiopians predominating. Largely a mountainous country, Yemen contains the highest elevations in Arabia. A range of mountains separates the narrow coastal plain on the west from a high plateau in the center and east. The plateau, which has a temperate climate, provides rich agricultural areas.

Until 1962 the nation was an autocratic monarchy based on Islamic law. Its leader, called the imam,[1] exercised tyrannical rule. In September of 1962 a military junta promoted a successful revolt and proclaimed the country a republic. Seven years later, fighting still continues. Rival forces occupy different sections of the country, though the cities are in the hands of the Republicans. Britain and her associates in the Commonwealth, along with most of the western European nations and the Latin American countries, continue to recognize the royalist regime. The United States, Russia, and most of the countries of the Communist bloc and of the Arab world (with the exception of Saudi Arabia) acknowledge the regime of the republic.

Until the summer of 1967 the United Arab Republic (Egypt) paid 90 percent of the Yemen republic's administrative budget. In return for this favor, Egypt was allowed to exert a controlling interest in the affairs of the country. In fact, the country was ruled from July of 1964 by a coordinating council of twelve members, six each from the Republic of Yemen and the United Arab Republic. In effect, Yemen was a satellite of the UAR.

Islam is the state religion in Yemen. Sixty percent of the people are Sunni Muslims and the remainder, including the royal family, are Shiites. Most of the country's 50,000 dark-skinned, oriental Jews have, since 1948, emigrated to Israel, where they have experienced some difficulty in integrating with Jews from other parts of the world.

Sana, the capital city, has an estimated population of 100,000. It is the communications center of Yemen, with an airport modernized in 1963. Gold and silver jewelry, some other handicraft industries, and a textile factory built with aid from Communist China give a degree of prosperity to the city.

Taiz was occupied by the Republican regime as its capital until 1964 when the capital became Sana. Until the rise of its neighbor, Aden, in the nineteenth century as the chief South Arabian port, Taiz was a busy trading center. In the fourteenth century an Islamic university, no longer extant, helped it to flourish as a great cultural city. Modern Taiz is a center for the agricultural produce of the district. Textile, leather, and jewelry handicrafts round out its economy. It has a population of about 80,000.

The nation's ports on the Red Sea are Hodeida with a population of some 55,000, and Mocha with 6,000. The main export is the famous Yemeni coffee, which takes its name from the smaller seaport town. The Mocha brand of coffee is highly rated in the Arab world.

Customs

Time.—The people of Yemen calculate the hours of their day from 6:00 A.M. and 6:00 P.M. Greenwich mean time, used by the rest of the world, means little to them. Until the inauguration of the republic, the nation was unique in persisting in its use of the Turkish calendar, a seventeenth-century compromise between the Christian and Muslim calendars.

Marriage.—Women are married very young, often before reaching puberty. Ancient heathen influences still prevail; an egg is broken on the threshold of the bridegroom's home as a symbol of fertility. Fireworks explode and lights flash to ward off evil spirits during the prolonged marriage ceremony. If it is the second marriage for the bridegroom, his right eye is covered for the occasion. For a third marriage, he will hood both eyes. Enamored by the kind, efficient service of a Spanish Baptist nurse at the clinic in Taiz, an old Yemeni Muslim asked her to be his wife. He assured her that she would live like a queen in his household because he already had three wives who would do all the work.

Divorce.—Divorce, the Muslim woman's nightmare, is even more simple for the male in Yemen than in other

Arab countries. With a simple statement that he no longer desires the company of his wife, he packs her off with her dowry, back to her father's home. Remarrying a divorced wife is a more complicated matter. Muslim law insists that she should have married another husband in the interim period.

Narcotics.—A close observation of Yemeni men who are sitting around enjoying each other's company while smoking narghile or hookah pipes[2] may reveal that some seem to be chewing tobacco. In all probability they are chewing a bitter herb with properties similar to those of cocaine and opium, though containing neither of these. Taken with a little sugar to offset the bitter taste, a plug of this narcotic may last for hours, giving a sensation of relaxation and serenity. Modern Western society, clamoring for legal recognition of its exotic LSD practice, is just catching up!

Food.—The national dish of Yemen consists of mutton stew served with a pungent, aromatic sauce. It is called *helba*. Scooped up with a piece of bread torn off a large pancake-shaped loaf, this food is eaten with the fingers of the right hand. Only the right hand is used for eating. The left, with which the Arab performs his ablutions, is considered impure. The writer was laughed at once when, at an Arab feast, he washed both hands in the basin that was passed around after the main course.

"Why do you wash your left hand?" was the laughing inquiry. "You will only use your right."

Enter Baptists

By the end of August, 1964, Dr. James Young, Jr., was on his way from Gaza to Yemen, with his wife, two daughters, and a Spanish Baptist nurse. They took up residence in Taiz, in the southern part of the country, and immediately set about establishing a medical clinic.

What induces a man comfortably situated in Gaza to leave his two oldest children behind for study in a boarding school in Alexandria, endure the rigors of a journey by freighter in the heat of summer through the Red Sea, and then to travel overland by dirt track to a place that, when mentioned in Western circles, requires an exploration into history and geography textbooks for its identification and location?

The question may be answered by an illustration used by historian Arnold J. Toynbee in an article in the September 18, 1966, issue of the *Daily Star,* a newspaper in Beirut, Lebanon. In the article he tells the story of a Scottish knight who was carrying King Robert Bruce's heart to be buried in Jerusalem. As the knight was passing through Spain he stopped to help his fellow Christians in a battle against the Moors. When the issue hung in the balance, the knight hurled the casket deep into enemy ranks and then battled so furiously to reach and recover it that he routed the enemy and made the Christians masters of the field.

Dr. Young and his associates have gone deep into the Arab world. Backed by the prayer support of faithful fellow Christians, they can win the battle for Christ in Yemen. What a thrill that Southern Baptists have the privilege of pioneering for Christ in a country bereft of any Christian witness for thirteen centuries! The people of Yemen will hear through dedicated witnesses like Dr. Young.

A prefabricated hospital erected at Jibla, thirty miles from the city of Taiz, is a symbol of the pioneer spirit that still motivates Christian missionaries. To its clinic and wards come turbaned Muslims of Yemen. The physical healing that is lovingly provided for them will surely open their hearts for the reception of the message of the One who, when he saw the multitudes without a shepherd, was moved with compassion for their physical and spiritual needs.

Notes

[1] "Imam" originally meant the leader of a caravan and, hence, figuratively a moral guide. The first imam was the prophet Muhammad.

[2] An Oriental pipe with a long flexible tube so arranged that it draws the smoke through water in a vase or bowl, thus cooling it.

5
Hearing Through
Diverse Channels

How shall they hear, these millions of people in the Arab world?

Today's missionary enterprise is evangelistic in its basic thrust but diverse in the various channels it uses for the extension of the kingdom of God among men. Hospitals, schools, publications, radio, and social welfare unite with, and supplement, the ministry of churches to bring the message of God's redeeming love to the largest possible number of people.

Educational Evangelism

One of the most effective means used to spread the saving truth of the gospel is the Christian school. Missionary and national teachers, through the testimony of their lives and the words spoken in Bible class and chapel service, can make the claims of Christ pertinent to their students.

Missionaries Anna Cowan, Maurine Perryman, and J. Wayne Fuller have seen God at work in two primary and two secondary schools in Jordan. Lives have been changed as the seed of the gospel has been faithfully sown in the hearts of the students. Outstanding Muslims, even some who are fanatically opposed to Christianity, will send their children to Christian schools because they recognize high educational and character-building standards. The eagerness of Arab youth for higher education provides a golden opportunity for laying strong Christian foundations through mission schools.

A Baptist school in Beirut, Lebanon, has classes from nursery through high school. It provides a program of education which, while complying with the requirements of the Lebanese educational system, incorporates Bible teaching designed to bring students to understand God's Word and his redemptive purpose for their lives. Over a period of fifteen years, Jim and Leola Ragland have seen the Beirut Baptist school grow from a one-class nursery school in a storeroom to a modern institution of which Baptists are justly proud. Nancie Wingo joined them five years ago to head up the English program as she seeks to inspire young people with her Christian testimony.

Year after year parents have patiently placed the names of their children on the waiting list for enrolment in Baptist schools. People from non-Christian backgrounds are fully aware of the risk they undertake in sending their children to mission schools that have refused to compromise in their presentation of the claims of Christ and in following up with contacts in the homes of students. Every home represented in the student body is visited, with an evangelistic purpose, at least once during the academic year. Muslims, Druses, Maronite Catholics, Greek Orthodox, and Evangelicals are some of the major religious groups of the Arab world represented in the student bodies. These do hear. Many of them respond. Proportionately more decisions for Christ are made by students in Baptist schools during revivals than by members of any other community.

Beauty Queen or Christian Witness

An outstanding former student of the Beirut Baptist School, one of the few coeducational high schools in the Arab world, was Lebanon's 1967 beauty queen. She is not a Christian believer. Missionaries serving in the school grieve that in her years as a student she remained aloof to the claims of Christ.

More outstanding in terms of Christian values are the beauty queen's brother and sister, Elie and Claudeen Talea, two of the most sincere teen-age witnesses for Christ to be found anywhere. While the family concentrated on the promotion of the oldest daughter in beauty contests, to the neglect of the other children, God's Spirit was at work in the lives of Elie and Claudeen. Often lonely and discouraged, these two students found comfort in the kindness shown them by their missionary counselors and the pastor of the Musaitbi Baptist Church, which adjoins the school.

Elie is a leader in his church's youth organizations, a witness wherever God gives him opportunity. On graduation from high school, he began working in the area of Christian publications. This may be another step in the direction of a full-time gospel ministry.

Claudeen became discouraged and dropped out of school for a year, but a visit to the Ajloun Baptist Hospital in Jordan gave her a renewed vision of what God could do with her life. Convinced that she can witness for her Master best in the field of medical service, she is back in school now, determined to qualify academically for nursing training at the hospital.

Expelled and Reinstated

Nicola was a transfer student from another school.

One of his friends had recommended the Baptist High School. He found classroom conditions vastly different from those he had experienced before. Cheating in examinations had been winked at by the other schools. In the Baptist school, after several warnings from teachers he was sent to the principal's office where he was kindly but firmly informed that he was no longer acceptable as a student. His ruddy complexion visibly paled, but the principal's tone of voice convinced him that a final decision to expel him had been taken.

With more sadness than rebellion, Nicola collected his books and went home. Two days later his mother, with tears in her eyes, came to intercede for her son. She asked that he be given one more chance. Who can resist the pleas of a weeping mother? He was received back under probation.

Before the end of the school year Nicola accepted Christ as his Saviour and testified openly to his fellow students of his new joy and purpose in life. But there was trouble for him at home. His parents rejoiced in the evident change in their son's life but were not willing that he should be baptized.

Nicola waited patiently until he graduated from high school and found a job. Financially independent of his family, he felt free to make his own decisions. He confessed his Lord publicly through baptism and joined the fellowship of the Musaitbi Baptist Church.

A Third-generation Baptist

Samir Atweh is a medical student at the American University of Beirut. Evident in his witness for Christ is something of the faithfulness of his paternal grandparents, who were among the earliest Baptist converts in Beirut, and something too of the dedication of his maternal grandparents, the Rev. and Mrs. Saleem Sharouk.

Samir was enrolled in the Beirut Baptist School as a second grader. When he was graduated from high school, he had the sixth highest marks among ten thousand students in the Lebanese Government baccalaureate examination (based on the French educational system). More important to him than his academic honors, Semir left high school knowing Christ in a personal way as Lord of his life.

At home and in Sunday School, Samir had been taught the Scriptures, which make a young man "wise unto salvation" (2 Tim. 3:15). The teaching and influence of the Baptist school complemented his home training so that his personal faith led him to turn over the direction of his life to Christ. Someday Samir will practice medicine and become probably the first national Baptist doctor in Lebanon.

The ministry of a Baptist mission school is being multiplied through Samir's witness today as a student in the largest American institution of higher learning outside the United States. By God's grace, his witness will be multiplied in the years ahead as he enters his lifework. Ten formative years in the Beirut Baptist School, during which the entire range of scriptural and Christian doctrine was taught, instilled in his mind supreme principles that give promise of a professional life dedicated to the glory and honor of Christ's name.

Baptist Publications

A long-term gospel ministry in the Arab world is made possible through a Baptist publications center in Beirut,

Lebanon. Its literature is being distributed in twenty-five countries from the Persian Gulf to the northwest African Atlantic coast, and even farther afield.

Early in her missionary service Virginia Cobb caught a vision of the possibilities of a publications ministry. Her talents in the difficult Arabic language have been used in the development of Arabic literature, from mimeographed Sunday School leaflets for Primary children to a variety of materials for the promotion of Baptist church work. They serve as an outreach to Arabic-speaking people who never enter a church.

Newspaper Evangelism

An exciting facet of the ministry of the Baptist publications center is newspaper evangelism. Fast aircraft speed Beirut dailies and weekly journals to every country of the Arab world. Brief, attention-catching articles appear in some of the most widely read newspapers and magazines. Readers are invited to write for counsel regarding their personal problems.

A wide response from persons of a variety of religious, educational, and professional backgrounds has been received. These provide opportunities for a follow-up ministry in which the printed page is used to present the claims of Christ to many who do not come under the direct influence of a pulpit ministry.

Correspondence Courses

A most fruitful ministry of the publications center in terms of response is that of the correspondence courses in which thousands are enrolled. Based primarily on the life of Christ, the courses are designed to initiate those who enrol into a systematic reading of the New Testament. Though widely advertised in the secular and religious press, the best publicity for the courses has come from people already enrolled who have recommended them to their friends.

"Please send me teaching about the Christian religion because I would like to increase my understanding of it and become a Christian man in the real sense of the word," wrote one inquirer in response to an advertisement of a correspondence course on the life of Christ.

Another said: "I noticed in one of the Lebanese newspapers your announcement about the life of Christ and found myself much inclined towards these valuable lessons because I am in great need of them to fill the emptiness of my soul."

"Please supply me with the lessons on the life of Christ," was another's plea, "because my soul is in the greatest need of spiritual life."

Someone from a non-Christian background expressed himself longingly: "After some study I would like to come to know the Lord Jesus Christ, for I have come to love him sincerely. Perhaps he will love me also!"

A group letter containing twenty-one signatures came from Hebron. It declared: "We are all friends and have met together and decided to study these lessons. And we have other friends who, when they see them, will request them also."

A high school student in Syria wrote that his teacher of religion in school told him about the lessons. A large number of requests for enrolment in the basic correspondence course have come from the same town.

From Baghdad came a scathing indictment of the slowness of Christians to witness: "I am a Muslim and very anxious to learn more about the Christian religion.

But Christians here in Iraq will not talk much with Muslims, and especially about religion, because they are afraid."

Still another wrote: "I have had some difficulty in answering your questions because I am a Muslim, twenty-two years old. For five years I have been trying to learn something about the life of Christ and the Christian religion because I discovered the love and brotherhood which every Christian feels for his brother. I found a book five years ago but my teacher took it from me. Please tell me of someone who can help me personally with my questions."

Five thousand correspondents are enrolled in these "Word of Life" courses. God has promised that his Word shall not return unto him void, but "shall prosper in the thing whereto I sent it" (Isa. 55:11).

The Power of the Printed Word

Hameed (meaning "worthy of praise") serves in the Baptist publications center in Beirut. His own conversion from Islam is a testimony to the power of the printed word.

Born into a Sunni Muslim family in Palestine, the youngest of four sons, he grew up with a keen religious bent. His father, a wicked man who in his early years was a trafficker in the narcotic called hashish and in other contraband, settled down after marriage. Determined to make amends for his wayward youth, he encouraged Hameed to study hard to prepare for the priesthood in the Muslim faith. To make it possible for Hameed to continue his studies, the three older brothers were sent to work after completing elementary school.

About ten years ago as Hameed, at that time a refugee

in Tyre, Lebanon, was studying one day in the open air by a well on the outskirts of the city, he was confronted by an evangelist who had come to the well to distribute tracts and to witness for Christ. Hameed was preparing for the government high-school examination.

"Can't you see I'm busy, studying?" Hameed said when the evangelist tried to speak to him. "Leave me alone."

The evangelist handed him a tract and said hurriedly, "God's Son will relieve your burden. He will give you peace."

Hameed stuck the tract in his shirt pocket and continued with his studies. That night before closing his eyes in sleep he began to think again of what the evangelist had said about Jesus: "God's Son will . . . give you peace." Hameed knew no real peace despite his attempts to fulfil faithfully his duties as a Muslim; but he had an important examination ahead of him and could not waste time thinking of what "that infidel Christian" had told him concerning "the Son of God."

"What utter blasphemy! Did God marry that he should have a Son?" Hameed thrust the evangelist's testimony from his mind. But the Holy Spirit began to convict him of sin.

After three days of struggle, he seemed to hear an inner voice saying to him, "Read the tract the evangelist gave you." Several times he felt the same impression and finally searched for the tract and read it. Its title was "What Shall It Profit?" What he read distressed him. He asked a nominal Christian friend if he knew where the evangelist who distributed tracts lived. His friend laughed and advised him to steer clear of that fanatic, but Hameed's persistence drew from him the general direction to the man's home.

Hameed found the evangelist sick with the flu but eager to talk with him. As the man spoke of Jesus the sin-bearer, he was surprised to hear Hameed declare, "If he can lift the burden of my sin I am ready to receive him now." Patiently the evangelist explained the plan of salvation and they knelt together as Hameed asked Christ to come into his heart and life.

Unable to hide his joy and peace, Hameed related his experience to his family. After the initial shock, his father ordered him out of the house. The evangelist's home became his refuge for a few days, and then he tried to return to his own family. His father beat him, the neighbors reviled him, and he was cast out again. On another occasion when Hameed tried to reestablish his relationship with his family his father suggested that they walk together along the seashore. As they walked and talked together and Hameed showed his determination to continue as a disciple of Jesus, his father drew a revolver and pointed it at his son's head. Suddenly his hand trembled violently and the gun fell harmlessly to the ground.

A few years later the father falsely accused his son of being a member of a banned political party that had attempted to overthrow the government. Several times the young man was imprisoned and beaten by soldiers trying to make him confess to the crime.

His faith has been tested in fiery trials, but has come forth purified and strengthened, a testimony to the saving and keeping power of God. He is a practical Christian. Despite all he has suffered from his family, he continues to send home monthly a portion of his earnings for his aging father's support. Concerning his loved ones, he can say with the apostle Paul that his "heart's desire and prayer" for them is that they too "might be saved" (Rom. 10:1).

While serving diligently at the Baptist publications center, Hameed continues his education on a part-time basis, taking courses at the Arab University in Beirut. His ambition is to earn the equivalent of a bachelor of arts degree.

How shall they hear? Some will hear, as Hameed did, through the printed word.

Publication Outlets

Two strategic outlets for Baptist publications are the Baptist bookstores in the cities of Amman and Jerusalem. These attractive shops provide an opportunity for tourists from the West to mingle with visitors from the Arab world. Arabs from every walk of life have come to inquire about spiritual matters.

After the mercifully short Jewish-Arabic war in the summer of 1967, there was a run on Arabic Bibles. People began to search the prophecies of the Old Testament, looking for some light to be cast on the complicated situation. A surprising number of the inquirers have talked with a sympathetic store manager about their deep spiritual hunger, which has not found satisfaction in their own traditional religion. They, too, may be introduced to Christ through the printed word or a personal witness given in a Baptist bookstore. Missionary Paul Smith, when he was manager of the stores in Jordan, seized a unique opportunity to present Bibles to a group of Arab Freemasons—merchants, professional men, and politicians—who represented a variety of nominal Christian and Muslim backgrounds. An alert missionary discovers many ways to spread God's Word.

Radio Ministry

A radio ministry is designed not to replace the ministry of the church, but rather to supplement it. However, it often does provide the only Christian witness in areas where there is no local congregation. In July, 1966, the Arab Baptist General Mission (organization of Southern Baptist missionaries serving in Gaza, Jordan, and Lebanon) was authorized to commence a radio ministry. As coordinator of this ministry, J. Conrad Willmon, with the help of a fellow missionary, David King, and a team of enthusiastic Arab nationals, is preparing programs for beaming to the entire Arabic-speaking world.

A well-equipped recording studio is located in the basement of the Arab Baptist Theological Seminary near Beirut, Lebanon. With medium-wave broadcasts to North Africa from stations in Europe and Africa and short-wave broadcasts for areas farther afield in the Arab world, recordings of the gospel message are being beamed to a potential audience of 100,000,000 people.

A Welfare Ministry

Missionary Mabel Summers is leading in a welfare ministry in the Karantina area of Beirut. Young people from a local Baptist church work faithfully with her and other missionaries to give the gospel to women, girls, and younger children of both sexes, through a combination of sewing and Bible study classes.

"Girls of Light" was the name adopted by the young women of the area for their organization. Their scriptural motto is "God is light, and in him is no darkness at all" (1 John 1:5). Bible verses are memorized by many who are illiterate. Bible stories are taught as simply as possible to a group who are responding to a ministry of loving concern.

No level of society can be neglected if the people of the Arab world are to hear the good news of salvation for all.

A Seminary Ministry for the Arab World

The training of God-called men and women is an important part of the missionary ministry to the Arab world. The number of missionary messengers of Christ being small, it is necessary to train nationals as pastors, evangelists, teachers, and church leaders. The writer, a missionary in Lebanon, commenced theological classes in his home in the fall of 1953 with three students. The classes continued for two years, with three additional students joining the group the second year. Missionary William Hern in Jordan began a similar ministry for eager students in 1956. This was continued for more than a year. But the dream of these missionaries was to establish a seminary for the entire Arabic-speaking world, with in-service training for those unable to attend.

The dream has become a reality. The seminary met for its first year of operation in 1960 in rented quarters in the city of Beirut. Lebanon was chosen as the best location for the school because of its religious freedom and political stability. Fifteen students were enrolled that first year.

During the following year the gifts of Southern Baptists through the Cooperative Program and the Lottie Moon Christmas Offering made possible the erection of buildings on a permanent campus near the village of Mansourieh in the foothills of the Lebanon Mountains. It is five miles from the city of Beirut, and its elevation is 750 feet higher.

To the classrooms of this modern "school of the prophets" have come students from Iraq, Syria, Lebanon, Jordan, and Egypt. Applications have come from Morocco, Mali, and the Sudan. Someday, turbaned students from Yemen will come here to study more about Christ. Regularly appointed missionaries have shared with nationals and with sabbatical-leave professors from the United States in the ministry of this school, which is designed to serve the entire Arabic-speaking world.

Joseph Ashkar was one of the first graduates of the seminary. His uncle was the leader of a prominent Lebanese political party, and the ambition of Joseph's father was that his son should be trained for a political career. Joseph's education was well planned and progressing favorably in the best school near the mountain resort town of Bikfaya where he grew up. But one day he crossed swords with his teacher and, in the heat of the argument, threw a textbook at him. When the boy refused to apologize for his conduct, he was expelled.

For days, Joseph roamed the streets while his friends attended school. One day he encountered a Baptist preacher who, seeing his disconsolate expression, inquired kindly about his condition. Joseph told his story, bitterly declaring that he would never return to that school again. The pastor expressed his sympathy and his regret that his church had no day school to offer. He invited Joseph to meet with a group of boys who came to his church on Sundays for Bible study. There, for the first time in his life, Joseph heard about Christ as a personal friend willing to fill the vacuum in a boy's life. Much to his father's annoyance, he continued to attend

Sunday School and the preaching services of the church.

New Year's Eve approached and Joseph went to the special watch-night service in the Bikfaya Baptist Church. As the few members thanked God for the blessings he had bestowed on them during the past year and dedicated themselves anew to his service in the new year, the pastor seized the opportunity to press the claims of Christ on all who were present. Noticing as he closed his message that Joseph was visibly moved, he tarried with the boy as the others left and spoke to him about his soul's need. Joseph had a foreboding of what confessing Christ would cost him. A mighty struggle was going on in his heart, but the grace of God triumphed. Kneeling with the pastor, he brokenly confessed his sins and accepted Christ into his life. His immediate joy was beyond description.

The time was past midnight. Joseph made his way home and was met at the door by his father. Without delay, he told his dad of his decision. The fury of his parent's anger was even more than he had expected.

"You have a choice to make," his father yelled at him. "If you are to continue as a member of this home you must give up your newfangled ideas and promise that you will cease to attend the services at the Baptist church."

"I have already decided to follow Jesus and I cannot turn back," said the sixteen-year-old boy as he turned away, tears in his eyes. Although banished from his home, he had the deep consciousness that Christ was with him. That night the pastor took him in.

Joseph eventually found work in Beirut, commuting fifteen miles daily by bus. The Lord prospered him as he worked and witnessed in the office of an oil industry supply company. He read his Bible and testified to his fellow passengers as he rode to and from work, and won several of them to Christ. All this time he was being prepared in a practical way for his life work, for God was calling him to special service. Hearing that Baptists were planning to open a seminary, he was one of the first to apply for entrance. His academic background was below standard, but his earnestness and sense of call were so evident that the admissions committee made an exception in his case and accepted him.

With no financial backing, Joseph was obliged to spend several hours of each day in manual labor in order to pay for his room and board. He accepted every task cheerfully and executed it joyfully. His diligence in study produced excellent results. After three years came the first graduation day of the Arab Baptist Theological Seminary. There was a hush of expectation as Joseph stepped up to receive his diploma and a burst of applause as the citation, "With Distinction," was read.

Today Joseph serves as the first home missionary of the Lebanese Baptist Convention, witnessing in a needy area in the north of the country. A disciplined life of prayer, a compassion for the lost, and a winsome personality are some of the qualities that have made him a successful soul-winner. The investment of Southern Baptists in training him for the gospel ministry is bringing forth multiplied fruit in the lives which he in turn reaches for Christ.

All of the Foreign Mission Board's missionaries serving around the world today would not adequately meet the need of the Arab world alone. To supply that unmet need, trained and dedicated graduates of the Arab Baptist Theological Seminary are being used of the

Lord throughout the Arabic-speaking world. They go not only into areas where missionaries are free to preach, but also—and especially—into areas where missionaries as such have no entrée. In increasing numbers, graduates of this school will be witnesses of God's truth to Arabic-speaking people, one of the major language groups of the world.

Egypt, an Arabic-speaking country, is closed to Baptist missionaries.[1] It's 30,000,000 people know little of the biblical message of God's redeeming love. How shall they hear?

A graduate of the Arab Baptist Theological Seminary serves as pastor of the Baptist church in Beni Suef, sixty miles south of Cairo. Other Egyptian students at the seminary are preparing for service in their homeland. The city of Cairo, with a population of more than four million, has one small Baptist church. The activities of Baptist missionaries in the land of the Pharaohs have been limited to irregular counseling visits, but Egyptian nationals who have gone to the Baptist seminary in Lebanon for training are welcome home. Through them, their fellow countrymen will hear—many for the first time—the message of salvation.

A Southern Baptist toehold in Libya has been possible only through an English-language ministry to American military personnel and oil-company officials. Tunisia and Algeria are virtually closed to the gospel message. Two Southern Baptist couples recently appointed for Morocco will have the responsibility for witnessing to more than ten million people. The combined efforts of Southern Baptist missionaries and their national brothers and sisters of the Arab world can make only a dent—or only a scratch—in the facade of this area.

How Shall They Hear?

Muslims are not lost merely because they have been born Muslims. We who claim to be Christians have failed to tell them of the only One who can save them. Islam has no Saviour to offer them. Persistently, the question demands an answer: How shall they hear? Only if we tell them.

In a past generation, Samuel Zwemer, called the Apostle to Islam—and no one better merits the appellation—stood in a missionary convention and pled for greater concern for the sons of Ishmael. In a heart-moving conclusion, he swept his hand across a huge map of the Muslim world, saying with intense emotion: "Thou O Christ, art all I want; and Thou O Christ, art all they want. What Christ can do for any man, He can do for every man."[2]

The same challenge must be renewed in this generation. The surrender of a Muslim soul to Christ is a miracle. Hospitals and schools, churches and preaching places, publications and radio, are channels God is using to multiply this miracle. These God-given channels await our personal participation and earnest cooperation that the millions of the Arab world may hear and believe and be saved.

Notes

[1] As this manuscript was cleared in December, 1968, for the press, a missionary family was making plans to move to Egypt early in 1969.—Ed.

[2] J. Christy Wilson, "The Epic of Samuel Zwemer," *The Muslim World*, LVII, No. 2 (April, 1967), 83.

The Author

Dr. Graham, a native of Greenock, Scotland, has been a missionary in Lebanon since 1948. Appointed in 1947, he served briefly in Nazareth, Palestine, and in Jordan. His work was general evangelism until 1960 when be became president of the Arab Baptist Theological Seminary near Beirut.

Mrs. Graham is the former Julia Saccar Hagood. They have four teen-age daughters: Catherine Mary, Rose Mary, Bertha Christine, and Sheila Ann. Mrs. Graham has a son, James Henry Hagood, Jr., by a former marriage.

Before his appointment as a missionary, Dr. Graham was a navigator in the Royal Air Force. He has the Master of Arts degree from Glasgow University and the Bachelor of Divinity and Doctor of Theology degrees from Southwestern Baptist Theological Seminary, Fort Worth, Texas.

THE EDITOR

Questions

Chapter 1

1. Who are the sons of Ishmael and in what part of the world do they live?
2. What three monotheistic faiths lay claim to the Holy Land?
3. Contrast the Koran's statement on retaliation with that found in the Gospel of Matthew.
4. Why is it difficult for a Muslim to become a Christian?
5. Why do Southern Baptist missionaries serve in lands where converts to Christianity are comparatively few?

Chapter 2

6. Name three unifying factors in Arabic culture.
7. Name and describe briefly the predominant religion of Arabs.
8. Describe at least three customs or habits that are about the same all over the Arab world.
9. How do Muslim marriage customs differ from those in the United States?
10. Name and identify the three main groups into which Arab people are divided.

Chapter 3

11. Who was the Lebanese photographer who began Baptist work in Lebanon?
12. When did Southern Baptist missionaries first serve in Palestine or the Holy Land?
13. In what ways is Lebanon unique among the Arab countries?

14. Identify the following: Druses, Maronites, Greek Orthodox.
15. From what religious background do most Arab Baptist church members come?

Chapter 4

16. In what Middle Eastern countries do Southern Baptists have hospitals?
17. Outline briefly the history of Baptist work in Ajloun.
18. What makes mission work in Gaza particularly difficult?
19. How long has Yemen been without a Christian witness?
20. Outline briefly the beginning of Baptist work in Yemen.

Chapter 5

21. List six channels through which missionaries carry the gospel to the Arab world.
22. Why are schools especially effective in Arab countries?
23. Describe three ways the publication center in Beirut, Lebanon, finds readers.
24. What progress have Southern Baptists made in a radio ministry to Arabs?
25. Where is the Arab Baptist Theological Seminary located?

Pronunciations

(Arabic sounds are indicated by the nearest sounds in English words or syllables.)

Abdul Messih /
  abd-DUL mess-SEEH
Aindara / ain-DAHR-ah
Ajloun / AZZ'h-loon
Aleppo / a-LEP-poh
Amman / am-MAN
Aqaba / OCK-ah-bah
Ayoub Naim / ah-YUBE
  nah-EEM

Baalbek / BAIL-beck or
  BALL-beck
Beirut / bay-ROOT
Bekaa / bick-KAH
Beni Suef / BANN-nee
  s'waif
Bikfaya / bick-FAH-yah
Boulos / BOO-lohs

Cairo / KIGH-roe

Dahir / DAH-her
Druse / drews

Elias Saleebi / ee-lee-AS
  sah-LEE-bee
Farhani / far-HANN-ey
Fatimah / FAH-tim-ah
fellahin / fell-ah-HEEN

hadar / HAD-ahr
Haddad / had-DAD
Hameed / hah-MEED
helba / HELL-bah
Hodeida / ho-DAY-dah

Ibrahim / ib-rah-HEEM
imam / eh-MAHM
Irbid / UR-bid

Jibla / JIBB-lah
Jubayl / juh-BILE

Kaaba / KAH-bah
Karantina / car-ann-TEE-
  nah
Kefr Mishky / KEFF-er
  MISH-ky

Khan Yunis / kahn YOU-ness

Kifringi / ka-FRINGE-ee

Kisshaya / kiss-HAY-yah

Liontes / lee-ON-tease

Mahmoud / MAH-mood

Mansourieh / man-soo-REE-yah

Mecca / MECK-uh

Medina / mad-DEE-nah

Mieh / MEE-yeh

Mocha / MOCK-ah

Musaitbi / muss-SIGHT-be

Nicola / NICK-oh-lah

Orontes / oh-RON-tease

qiblah / KIBB-lah

Ramadan / ram-ah-DAWN

Richaya el Wadi / rah-SHAY-yah ell WAH-dee

Rizcallah / rizz-CALL-ah

Said Jureidini / sah-EED jur-ray-DEE-nee

Saleem Sharouk / sah-LEEM sha-ROOK

Samir Atweh / sam-EAR AHT-weh

Sana / son-NAH

Shiite / SHE-ite

Shubra / SHOE-bra

Talal Sheiban / tah-LAL shy-BANN

Wadia / wad-DEE-ah

Wardi / war-DEE

Yemen / Yemmen

Yusuf Daoud / YOU-suff (DAH-wood)

Zerka / ZEHR-kah

First Baptist Church
1717 St. Cloud Highway
St. Cloud, Florida 32769